WHAT IS PRAYER?

HOW TO PRAY TO GOD THE WAY YOU TALK TO A FRIEND

CHRISTIAN QUESTIONS
VOLUME 1

WHAT IS PRAYER?

HOW TO PRAY TO GOD THE WAY YOU TALK TO A FRIEND

J. D. MYERS

RedeemingPress.com

WHAT IS PRAYER?
How to Pray to God the Way You Talk to a Friend
© 2017 by J. D. Myers

Published by Redeeming Press
Dallas, OR 97338
RedeemingPress.com

ISBN: 978-1-939992-50-5 (Paperback)
ISBN: 978-1-939992-51-2 (Mobi Kindle)
ISBN: 978-1-939992-52-9 (ePub)

Learn more about J. D. Myers by visiting RedeemingGod.com

Cover Design by Taylor Myers
TaylorGraceGraphics.com

JOIN JEREMY MYERS AND LEARN MORE

Take Bible and theology courses by joining Jeremy at
RedeemingGod.com/join/

Receive updates about free books, discounted books,
and new books by joining Jeremy at
RedeemingGod.com/reader-group/

TAKE THE ONLINE COURSE
ABOUT PRAYER

There is an online course related to this book.
The audio lessons and downloads in the course
will help you learn more about prayer
and might also serve as a good small group Bible study.
Learn more at RedeemingGod.com/Courses/

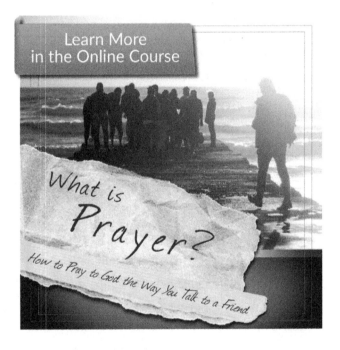

The course is normally $197, but you can
take it for free by joining the Discipleship Group at
RedeemingGod.com/join/

Other Books by Jeremy Myers

Nothing but the Blood of Jesus

The Atonement of God

The Re-Justification of God: A Study of Rom 9:10-24

Adventures in Fishing (for Men)

Christmas Redemption

Why You Have Not Committed the Unforgivable Sin

The Gospel According to Scripture (Forthcoming)

The Gospel Dictionary (Forthcoming)

Tough Texts on the Gospel (Forthcoming)

The Bible Mirror (Forthcoming)

The Grace Commentary on Jonah (Forthcoming)

Nin: A Novel (Forthcoming)

Studies on Genesis 1 (Forthcoming)

Studies on Genesis 2–4 (Forthcoming)

God's Blueprints for Church Growth (Forthcoming)

The Armor of God: Ephesians 6:10-20 (Forthcoming)

Books in the *Close Your Church for Good* Series

Preface: Skeleton Church

Vol. 1: The Death and Resurrection of the Church

Vol. 2: Put Service Back into the Church Service

Vol. 3: Church is More than Bodies, Bucks, & Bricks

Vol. 4: Dying to Religion and Empire

Vol. 5: Cruciform Pastoral Leadership (Forthcoming)

All books are available at Amazon.com

Learn about each title at the end of this book

This book is dedicated to
a close friend who is always there
to listen when I am happy, angry, or sad,
a confidant who never breaks trust
no matter how dark the secret I share,
and a counselor who never judges
my deepest doubt, sin, or fear.

This book is dedicated to God.

Thank you, Father, for listening, loving, and never leaving.

TABLE OF CONTENTS

FOREWORD

I remember when I was new to the Christian faith. I was unable to wrap my head around the sacred practice of prayer. Others had God on speed-dial while God's number always seemed to be changing for me. Over the years, doubts and questions kept piling up.

I didn't understand why we had to be so loud. Is God deaf? Does God consider us more spiritual if we are passionate and yell our prayers to Him? I didn't understand why we repeated God's name over and over again as if we were going into a trance-like state. Or did God forget His name?

I didn't understand what posture I needed to take for God to accept my prayers. Would God hear me better if I were on my knees? Would God like my prayers more, or even be fonder of me as His child, if I raised my hands?

And why did friends' prayers for God to give them parking spots at malls and convenience stores get answered, but not mine for my ailing and addicted mother? Is God cruelly selective in answering prayer?

I had tons of questions. Those haunting questions

kept me stuck, stagnant, and stale in my prayer life. Where was J. D. Myers' book *What is Prayer?* when I needed it?

I consider it an incredible privilege and honor to write a few words in support of this superbly written and enlightening book. J. D. Myers tackles the complexity and conundrum of prayer with a pastoral and prophetic heart, a brilliant and wise mind, and a courageous spirit obviously in touch and in tune with both God and God's people.

The good news is there is no conundrum in how to pray to God—at least not anymore. J. D. Myers sheds the religious and superstitious garb off of prayer and makes a simple, provocative, and liberating claim: Prayer is talking to God as you would talk to a friend.

I highly recommend this book not only to new Christians who want to learn how to pray but also to the experienced and inquisitive God-lover who still has many questions. Thank you, J. D., for such a gift to the Christian community!

Mark Karris
Author of *Divine Echoes: Reconciling Prayer with the Uncontrolling Love of God*
MarkGregoryKarris.com

INTRODUCTION TO THE "CHRISTIAN QUESTIONS" BOOK SERIES

This "Christian Questions" book series provides practical down-to-earth answers to everyday Christian questions. The series is based on questions that people have asked me over the years through my website, podcast, and online discipleship group at RedeemingGod.com. Since thousands of people visit the site every single day, I get scores of questions emailed in to me each month from readers around the world. Many of the questions tend to be around various "hot topic" issues like homosexuality, violence, and politics. Other questions, however, focus more on how to understand a particular Bible passage or theological issue. For example, I receive hundreds of questions a year about the unpardonable sin in Matthew 12.

I love receiving these questions, and I love doing my best to answer them. But after I answered the same question five or ten times, I realized that it might be better if I had a ready-made and easily-accessible resource I could invite people to read.

So the goal of this "Christian Questions" book series is to answer the questions that people send in to me. At this time, I do not know how many books will be in the series.

Below is the current list of books in the "Christians Questions" series. Most of these are not yet published, but I include the list to show you where the series is headed.

What is prayer?

Why is the world so messed up?

Can God forgive my sin?

What is the unforgivable sin?

What is baptism?

What is the church?

What is repentance?

How can I evangelize?

What is faith?

Can I lose eternal life?

Why did Jesus have to die?

Should Christians keep the Sabbath?

What is demon possession?

How can I gain freedom from sin?

What is election and predestination?

Does God love me?

Why did God give the law?

Does God really want blood sacrifices?

What is sin?

What is the best bible translation?

Can I trust the Bible?

How can I study the Bible?

If you have a question about Scripture, theology, or Christian living that you would like answered, you may submit it through the contact form at RedeemingGod.com/about/ or join my online discipleship group at RedeemingGod.com/join/.

Some of these "Christian Question" books are available as free PDF downloads to people who join my online discipleship group.

Visit RedeemingGod.com/join/ to learn more and join today.

CHAPTER 1

HOW TO TALK WITH GOD

Whether you pray or don't pray, whether you act or don't act, our relationship is still there—and ultimately that's all that counts. "But if you can manage it," God adds, "it will be a whole lot more fun if we can keep the conversation going."
—Robert Farrar Capon
Health, Money, & Love

A young pastor fresh out of seminary was leading his first service in his new church out in the country. Due to many years of studying Scripture and a head filled with theological knowledge, he viewed himself to be quite spiritual while the uneducated members of his congregation were somewhat backwards. So he decided that during his first service he would show the people what *real* prayer sounded like. He wanted to show them how spiritual he truly was. So after welcoming the congregation, he invited them all to bow their heads for the opening prayer. Then he launched into a long, eloquent, flowery prayer, full of big theological terms and allusions to Scripture. As this prayer went on and on, and as both children and adults started to fidget and look around at each other, one wee little woman in the choir decided to take the matter in hand. When the pastor paused to take a breath, she hollered out, "Jes' call 'im Father, an' ask 'im fer somethin'!"

This is a humorous story, but sadly, the pastor's prayer far too often reflects what goes on in Christian churches and Bible studies around the world. More tragically still, most churches don't have a brave little ol' lady in the choir to call out the pastor on his superspiritual, self-righteous prayer. So people go through life not knowing how to pray.

Many Christians don't know what to say in prayer. They don't know how to address God, whether or not to use "King James English" with "Thee's" and "Thou's," how long the prayer should be, and what sort of prayer requests to include. When they hear the "professionals" pray, such as the pastors, priests, and seminary professors, they think to themselves, "There is no way I could ever sound like that when I pray!" And since they think they don't know how to pray, they just don't pray. Even among those who do pray, there are many bad habits which get picked up along the way.

WHAT PRAYER IS NOT

Most people learn to pray by listening to others pray.

We learn how to pray, not by thinking about prayer or learning from Scripture about prayer, but by watching and listening to others pray. And frankly, we learn some very bad prayer practices this way.

For example, when some people pray, they seem to think that prayer requires a spiritual tone of voice, a new set of words, a sing-songy cadence and rhythm, with a repetition of certain words or phrases. So it is not uncommon to hear people pray this way:

> *Father God in heaven, holy art thou above all things, and thy name, Father God, is worthy to be praised, Father God. Hallelujah! Praise Your name, Jesus!*

> *Oh, Father God, Lord God, Holy Jesus, we come before you today, as your children, Father God, to beseech you with our many needs, Father God. But before we do so, oh Holy Father in Heaven, Father God, we ask thee to forgive us for our many sins. We have failed thee in so many ways, Father God, so that as the prophet Isaiah says, all our righteous works are as filthy rags before thee, Father God!*

> *And so we thank thee for sending thy holy Son, Jesus Christ, Father God, the Lord of the universe and the master of all, Father God, the Lamb who was slain before the foundation of the world, Father God, to die for our sins on that wretched cross, oh holy Father God. Hallelujah!—Praise Jesus—So that we might be forgiven of our many trespasses against you, Oh Holy Father God …*

And the prayer goes on this way for many minutes.

Is this prayer? Many seem to think so, since this type of praying is rather common in some Christian churches. This sort of cadence praying will differ from church to church and from person to person, so that there will be different rhythms that get followed and words that get repeated, but the basic approach is the same. I have heard some people start throwing in biblical Hebrew or Greek words, while others switch back and forth between English and speaking in tongues. But ask yourself: Would you ever talk to anyone else in such a fashion? If not, then why do we talk to God this way? Do we think this is what He expects or demands?

Occasionally, people will start talking to Satan during these prayers as well:

> *Father, we thank you for your presence here today, and for the fellowship of the saints we feel in this room, and Satan, we cast you out in the name of Jesus! Flee this place because we are washed in the blood of the Lamb! And God, may the words that we sing and the prayers of our hearts be holy unto you this day. Get thee behind, me, Satan! So we pray, God, for Pastor Tom as he brings the Word today …*

When I hear prayers like this, I often wonder who the person is praying to, God or Satan? I sometimes wonder if God gets frustrated as well that we are allowing Satan to butt into a conversation we are supposed to be having with God. God is probably saying, "Satan's gone! Now talk to Me; not him."

Sometimes the bad habits we have in prayer are not so much about the words we say, but about the proper posture of prayer. For example, it is not uncommon for churches to teach, especially to children, that the proper way to pray is with head bowed, eyes closed, and hands folded. This, of course, helps keep the children from fidgeting and talking during prayer, but we must ask what exactly we are telling children about God if we teach them that in order to talk to God, they have to sit and act a certain way.

There are numerous other types of bad habit prayers, and maybe none of the examples above match your own prayer patterns. But even if you do not pray the way I have written above, listen to yourself pray sometime, and ask yourself, "Where did I learn how to pray this way?" Why am I saying these certain words? Why am I changing my voice? Why am I bowing my head and folding my hands? Why do I pray to Jesus or to the Holy Spirit? Why do I repeat this certain phrase over and over?" Asking these sorts of questions will help you discover any bad prayer habits of your own.

The goal, of course, is not just to discover bad prayer habits, but to break these habits and learn to really pray as God wants and desires. Thankfully, learning to pray properly is quite simple. It all begins by simply understanding what prayer is.

WHAT PRAYER IS

When we come to understand prayer, we are able to almost instantly break most of our bad habits about prayer. When we truly understand how to pray, most of our questions and uncertainty about how to pray simply fade away. When we understand what prayer is, we lose our fear of praying and discover that we already know how to pray.

So what is prayer?

I am not even going to try to get technical and fancy with my explanation. Being a Bible scholar, I was tempted to break out the Greek and the Hebrew and pull out my big stack of books, but that would then defeat the purpose of showing you how simple prayer is, and how you can have confidence that you are praying the "right" way. So in trying to answer the question, "What is prayer?" the simplest and most practical answer is best.

So what is prayer? Prayer is simply talking to God as you would talk to anyone else. Prayer is having a conversation with God. If you know how to talk to people, then you also know how to talk to God. That's it! If you want to put the book down now, you can. If you know how to have a conversation, then you know how to pray. There is nothing magical or mysterious about prayer. Prayer is nothing more than talking to God as you would talk to a friend.

I suppose I should qualify that last statement. Although prayer is "nothing more" than talking to God, it is certainly nothing less! I don't want you to miss how shocking the gift of prayer actually is. Prayer allows you to talk to *God* as you would talk to a friend! You can talk to God more easily and more readily than you can talk to the President of the United States. Prayer allows you to start up a conversation with God, the creator and ruler of the universe. There is no idea more shocking. That God would be so friendly and make Himself so available to us is amazing.

I hope that this truth doesn't make you more nervous about prayer, but rather more amazed. God has made Himself available to you all the time about anything. You do not need a priestly mediator, or special words, or a holy language, or a spiritual frenzy in order for God to pay attention to you. All such things are *religious* trappings that do nothing but get in the way of actual communication with God.

Mark Karris has defined prayer similarly, and in his book on prayer, he writes this:

> Prayers are not magical incantations or secret coded messages wrapped in sacred energy. To pray simply means *to talk to God.* Try this thought experiment. Let's assume you have been praying for your ailing mom. Repeat this sentence out loud: "I have been *praying* that God heals my mom." Now say, "I have been *talking to* God about healing my mom." ... Simply substituting "praying" with

"talking" has the potential to reduce thinking that views prayer as some magical incantation or other form of superstition while increasing the relational component of prayer.[1]

PRAYING LIKE MOSES

It is quite common for Christians to be jealous of the relationship that Moses had with God. In Exodus 33:11, we are told that God spoke to Moses, as a man speaks to a friend. And we think, "Wow! Imagine having such a close relationship with God! It would be so nice to speak to God like I speak to one of my friends. I could tell Him anything. I could talk to Him at any time. I wouldn't have to worry about using the right words. How I long for this type of prayer!"

Guess what? You have it! The Bible doesn't tell us what kind of friendship Moses had with God so that we could be jealous of Moses, but instead to show us what kind of friendship all of us have with God, if we simply take advantage of it. This is exactly what the Apostle John writes in 1 John 1:3. After basically saying, "Hey, I know all of you reading this wish that you could have been an Apostle, seeing what Jesus did, hearing Jesus teach, and hanging out with Jesus over a meal. Well,

[1] Mark Gregory Karris, *Divine Echoes: Reconciling Prayer with the Uncontrolling Love of God* (Orange, CA: Quoir, 2018), 24. This book is not yet available, but Mark Karris was gracious enough to send me a pre-release version. As a result, the page numbers will likely be different than those cited here.

Jesus is my friend, and I am writing this letter to tell you how you and I can be friends. This means that if you are my friend, and I am Jesus' friend, then you are friends with Jesus too. Let me show you how." And John goes on to give some really practical advice on how to remain in fellowship (friendship) with Jesus, with God, and with one another. John ends his letter talking about prayer, where he basically says, "So just boldly talk to God. When you talk to God, He hears you, because He's your friend" (1 John 5:14).

Earlier in his letter, John wrote that we can love God and love others because God first loved us (1 John 4:7-8). By writing about how to love and be loved, John reveals that God is our friend, that God loves us, and that God wants to be in a close friendship with us. The greatest proof of this, John says, is that God sent Jesus into the world (1 John 4:9-10). This means that you are so important to God, He is dying (literally) to talk with you. You don't need to be scared of talking to God, or nervous about what to say. Just talk to God the way you talk to a friend who thinks only good things about you.

JUST TALK TO GOD

Do you want to learn how to pray? Do you want to know what to pray for? Do you want to know how long to pray and where to pray? The answers to all such questions are answered by simply asking the same questions about a friend. Do you know how to talk to a friend? Of course. It's easy. It's natural. It's normal. Do you worry about what to talk to your friend about? No. That's one reason they are a friend. It is not even uncomfortable to sit in silence with a good friend. Do you worry about how long you should talk to a friend? No. Sometimes the conversations are long; sometimes they are short. The length of the conversation doesn't matter when you're talking to a friend. Do you worry about where you are going to talk to your friend, or how you are going to sit, or what words you should say? No! These are not of any concern when you are talking to a friend.

One more beautiful thing about talking to God as a friend is that He is always with you. He is always paying attention and always there. He is with you throughout the day, going where you go, doing what you do, and hanging out with you as you eat, as you work, as you drive. Even as you sleep! But not in a creepy way.

The bottom line is that if you want to learn how to pray, all you need to do is talk to God as you would talk to a friend. Tell God what is going on in your life. Keep Him in the loop. Are you angry? Tell God. Are you sad? Let Him know! Did you see something beautiful or experience something joyful? Thank Him! Do you have needs and concerns? Ask Him for advice or help. Did you just sin? Well, He saw it, and He is not mad, but He does want to talk to you about it. He may even want to laugh with you about your sin. I know that this goes against the traditional Christian view of sin as being a terrible affront to God, but when I talk to God about my sin, I have often found that rather than scowling at me with stern eyes and folded arms, He tends to have a sparkle in His eyes and a half-smile on His lips. He chuckles and says, "I can't believe you fell for that *again*!" Then we talk about what happened and how to avoid it in the future.

Do you see how no matter what is going on in your life, God wants to be part of it and communicate with you about it?

But what if you are the silent type? What if you are a person of few words? What if you have trouble talking to anyone about anything, including your friends? That's okay too! God is absolutely fine with just sitting in your presence as you do whatever it is you're doing. You might say five or ten words to Him throughout the day, but He's fine with that, because it is who you are (and who He made you to be). Of course, if, on the other hand, you are a chatterbox and can talk to anyone about anything, that's great with God. Go ahead and include Him in your unending stream of words. (Don't take offense! You know who you are! Embrace it!) Whoever you are and whatever your conversation style, include God in the mix and just talk to Him as you would anyone else. Since your relationship with God already exists, and since you are already walking with God through life, you might as well make your journey more enjoyable by talking with God along the way.

One word of caution though. As you go about your day, talking to God whenever, wherever, and about whatever, you might want to keep your prayer life as an inner dialogue. Otherwise, if you talk out loud to God while you shop at the supermarket or work at your job, people will think you're crazy. The great thing about talking to God as a friend is that He knows your thoughts as well.

CONCLUSION

God wants to be real to us, and for that to happen, we need to be real with Him. He doesn't want fake religiosity, either in our lives or in our prayers. So be who you are and talk to God as you would talk to anyone else. Do not feel that you need a special prayer voice, special prayer words, or a special prayer posture. Feeling that you need such things will usually only get you in trouble.

I once sat through a church service that concluded with communion. A relatively inexperienced person was invited to offer the prayer for the communion. So he came to the front, picked up the communion bread and held it high in the air above his head. Then he began to pray. "Oh Lord!" he shouted. "We have gathered here in thy presence, and we thank thee for this holy bread, the fruit of thy loins ..." I did everything I could to not break out laughing. Needless to say, I did not partake of communion that day, for I could not remove from my head the image of bread coming from the loins of God. This man's prayer was genuine, but he also was trying to use words and terminology that he had heard elsewhere but didn't understand. And so he ended up thanking God for how we were going eat the fruit of His loins.

Another time, I was discipling a brand new Christian. He knew nothing about God, Jesus, Scripture, or church, and had never even heard anyone pray except for me. After our discussion one day, I asked him if he wanted to pray. He had heard me pray, and so knew that it was just like talking to anyone else, and so he agreed. Being the rough character that he was, this is what he said in his prayer:

> Hey God, you know I've f***** up a lot in life. Thanks for Jeremy helping me learn all this s*** from the Bible about Jesus and how you love and forgive me. Help me to remember what I'm learning and not f*** up anymore. Thanks … Amen.

After he finished praying, he looked at me and said, "How was that?" I smiled at him and said, "It was perfect. And God loved it too." And I am certain God did. It was honest. It was real. Best of all, it was exactly how this man talked to his friends. As this man matured in his faith, I knew that God would eventually go to work on his language, but for now, God just enjoyed that this new child of His was talking to Him as a friend.

So what is prayer? It is simply talking to God in a normal way, just as we talk to anybody else. Since this is the case, this means that you don't really need to read books on prayer. Not even the rest of this one. You don't need to be taught *how* to pray. You don't need to attend prayer training seminars. You don't need to learn a prayer language. You don't need to memorize lots of Scripture in order to pray. You don't need to learn Hebrew. If you know how to talk, you can pray! All you need to do is just imagine God sitting next to you, and talk to Him as you would talk to anyone else.

Do you want to pray? Aside from the fact that you are talking to *God*, prayer is nothing special. "Jes' call 'im Father, an' ask 'im fer somethin'!" Talk to Him as you would talk to anyone else, and your prayers will be just fine.

But what is it you should ask God for? This is the question we consider next.

CHAPTER 2

WHAT SHOULD YOU PRAY FOR?

It is one thing to know what prayer is. It is quite another knowing what to pray for. We all, of course, want to "pray according to the will of God," so that our prayers can be heard and answered. And so lots of people have developed various systems and suggestions over the years for teaching Christians what to pray for. These range from prayer cards and prayer lists to praying through acronyms such as ACTS: Adoration, Confession, Thanksgiving, and Supplication. Many people also recommend praying through Scripture.

I am not opposed to any of these ideas and suggestions. If they work for you, use them. I would, however, propose that all such prayer systems run the risk of taking you away from what we learned in the previous chapter, that prayer is nothing more than simply communicating with God. If prayer is simply communicating with God, then you don't need cards, lists, acronyms, or memorized passages to talk with God any more than you need such things to talk to your spouse, your children, your neighbor, or a coworker. I do not know anyone who maintains a "conversation topic list" for what they want to say when they talk to other people. So why would you use such things to talk to God? If such a list would make conversation with people unnatural, then it also makes conversation with God unnatural.

I do actually know of one person who used a "topic list" to talk to another person. It was me. I was in Junior High and there was a girl in our church's youth group that I really liked. But I was terrible at talking with girls, so I decided that if I was going to talk to her, I needed to come up with a list of topics beforehand to help me through a conversation. So I wrote up a list of about ten items on a 5x7 notecard. Then I sneakily put the notecard in a see-through pocket of my Bible so that if I started talking to her at church, I could glance at the notecard in the pocket of my Bible without her knowing that I was getting cues from my card.

The next Sunday I got the opportunity to use my card. She was standing around after the service, so I went up and launched into my "conversation." Much to my dismay, she was much less interested in my ten conversation topics than I was, and I blew through all ten in about two minutes. Then I had nothing left to talk about. So I stood there awkwardly for another few seconds, and then said, "Well, okay. Bye!" and walked off. I sometimes wonder if she still remembers that conversation as being the strangest conversation she has ever had in her life. More likely than not, she forgot all about it five minutes later.

The point is that cue cards and topic lists are only marginally helpful in having a conversation with someone else, and might actually be more detrimental than beneficial. This is not only true when you engage people in conversation, but also when you engage God in conversation. Just as conversation lists and cue cards are unnatural in normal conversations, so also, they can be detrimental to your conversations with God. When prayer becomes natural and normal, you discover that like any other conversation, you can carry it out all day long.

Nevertheless, it is true that initially, it is awkward to talk with God. We are afraid of saying the wrong thing or don't know what to talk to Him about. But once again, this is exactly how it is when you first start developing a friendship with anyone else. Initial conversations are nearly always awkward as you both struggle to find areas of common interests and topics that both of you are knowledgeable and passionate about. Of course, with God, He knows all things and is passionate about all things, and so He is happy to talk about whatever is on your mind or whatever interests you. But still, for the person who is just starting out, it is helpful to have some conversation starters. Some ice breakers are helpful in any conversation, especially when it's a conversation with God.

So in this chapter, we are going to briefly look at what many call "The Lord's Prayer" in Matthew 6:9-13 and Luke 11:2-4. This prayer is not actually "The Lord's Prayer" because Jesus is not actually praying. Instead, He is simply giving His disciples some suggestions on what to pray for when they communicate with God the Father. So for this reason, it is better to call this "The Disciples' Prayer" or "The Model Prayer." It provides a model, or framework, for disciples of Jesus to follow when they communicate with God. Let us look at what Jesus tells His disciples about communicating with God.

THE DISCIPLES' PRAYER

The most surprising thing about the suggested "prayer requests" that Jesus provides to His disciples is that every single one of these requests has the potential to turn your life upside down. There are no mundane prayer requests in the prayer that Jesus instructs His disciples to pray. Each line of this prayer is designed to invite God to overthrow, upend, and destroy your life. When you talk to God about the items in this model prayer, God enters your life like a bull in a china shop and tears everything down.

Afterwards, of course, God takes the shards of crystal glass scattered all over the ground and, from these shards, makes the most beautiful mosaic you have ever seen. This truth is taught all over the Scripture. If you want God to work in your life through prayer, the beginning stages of God's work will feel an awful lot like destruction. But if you bear with Him through the demolition, He will raise your life up from the ashes and rubble into something far better than you could ever ask or even imagine. The truth we see in the prayers of Jesus and the pages of Scripture is that death precedes resurrection. This is something to be aware of as you listen to Jesus about how to pray.

Before we look at His instructions, though, note that this model prayer from Jesus is not a prayer to be memorized and recited. You have not prayed the Disciple's Prayer if you mindlessly recite the words of this prayer once or twice a day. I once stayed overnight with a family where the children had been taught to recite this prayer before bed. As the children climbed into bed, their father said, "Don't forget to say your prayers!" The children knelt at their beds and said this:

OurFatherwhoartinheavenhallowedbythyname thykingdomcomethywillbedoneonearthasitisinheaven giveusthisdayourdailybreadandforgiveusourtresspasses asweforgivethosewhotresspassagainstus leadusnotintotemptationbutdeliverusfromevil forthineisthekingdomandthepowerandthegloryforever- amen.

It took them all of ten seconds. Then they climbed into bed having said their "prayers." But this is not why Jesus gave us this prayer. It is not simply a set of words to memorize so that you know exactly what to say when you pray, and the quicker you get it over, the better. No, Jesus taught this prayer to show the sorts of things you can say to God when you are in a conversation with Him. The Disciple's Prayer provides a few conversation topics to get you started. But these are not the only topics you can talk to God about. Since prayer is a conversation with God, you can talk to Him about anything that is on your heart and mind.

Below is a quick summary of how each line in the Disciple's Prayer will upend, overturn, and destroy your life as you know it. I am using the prayer found in Matthew (Matt 6:9-13) because it is familiar to most people.

Our Father in heaven

Praying to God as our Father is revolutionary in itself. Many people view God as a Ruler or King who sits on His throne and stares down at us as we grovel at His feet. But Jesus invites us to think of God as our Father, and to speak to Him as a loving, caring Father. Don't think of God as a high and lofty Judge, staring at you with a scowling face. Instead, think of God as a strong, kind, and caring man who loves to chat with you about life and share His wisdom as the two of you take a walk in the country, go for a drive into the city, or watch the football game. He is the man who wants to hear about your day and is genuinely interested in everything you say.

As a side note, many people pray to Jesus or to the Holy Spirit. This is not necessarily wrong, since prayer is simply a conversation, and we can have conversations with Jesus and with the Holy Spirit. Nevertheless, don't neglect your ongoing conversation with God, your Father, for when Jesus told us what to pray for, He instructed us to direct our prayers to God, our Father.

Hallowed be Your Name

This is a declaration that we want God's name to be glorified. When you pray, tell God that you want to let people know how amazing He is. The danger in this is that when we pray for God to be glorified, and for His name to be praised among the people, what we often subconsciously mean is that we want *our* name to be praised and glorified among people. Oh sure, when this happens, we imagine how we will stand in front of the adoring crowds and point our finger to heaven saying, "Give God the glory!" while we bask in the glory for ourselves. Yes, we want God to be gloried, but we often want to ride His coattails to some glory of our own.

But Jesus doesn't say this will happen. This first prayer item is for God's name to be glorified; not ours. And if Scripture is any guide, God often chooses the strangest ways to glorify His name. He uses shepherds, children, and donkeys more than the rich, powerful, and popular. So while it is okay to expect that God will glorify His name through you, just know that God's movement toward glory might involve a lot of downward momentum for yourself. When you follow God toward glory, you are more likely to be led toward obscurity and poverty than toward riches and fame.

Your kingdom come, Your will be done, on earth as it is in heaven

To pray for God's kingdom to come means to pray for God's will to be done. The concepts are one and the same. The Kingdom of God is the rule and reign of God, and so when God is ruling and reigning, His will is being done. This means that when you talk to God, make it plain that you want to be involved in helping Him carry out His plans and desires on this earth. This is what it means to pray for His will to be done. And this is something we all want, right? Some people even include the phrase "Not my will, but Yours be done" in their prayers (following the example of Jesus in Luke 22:42).

But again, this is a dangerous thing to say to God, for while you might be fine with God carrying out His will on earth, it is quite another thing when God steps into your life and starts trying to change your plans, your goals, and your dreams. We are usually fine with God carrying out His will in the lives of other people, as long as He doesn't mess up *our* life. If you are like me, when it comes to our own life, we want our own will to be done; not God's. Why? Because God's will for our life usually looks much less enjoyable than our own plans for our life. Following God's will for our life will lead us into death, slavery, obscurity, and suffering, rather than into riches, fame, honor, and glory.

But have courage and faith. God's plan truly is better, though it may not initially appear to be so. Note that the final statements of this prayer in verse 13 contain the same sort of ideas that Jesus states here. The Kingdom of God is God's rule and reign on earth, and it arrives by His power and is for His glory.

Give us this day our daily bread

Don't read more into this prayer item than is here. This is a request for God to provide for your daily needs. This is encouraging, because it once again shows that God wants you to talk to Him about what you have on your heart. Or in this case, God wants you to talk to Him about what you do *not* have in your stomach. So yes, you can talk to God about your need for food. Though it is not just about food, but also about our other physical, social, medical, financial, and psychological needs. You can talk to God about anything that concerns you.

So how is this a dangerous prayer? Well, note that Jesus only mentions *daily* bread. Daily bread means "enough for today." This is not a prayer for a full fridge and a growing retirement account. It is not a prayer for job security or financial freedom. For most of us, this is a terrifying prospect. If you are like me, you trust God for today and you trust God for tomorrow, but for your own peace of mind, you would like tomorrow's provision today. So if that is how you feel, go ahead and talk to God about it. If it is a concern you have today, He wants to hear about it.

And forgive us our debts, as we forgive our debtors

There is some question here about whether Jesus is talking about sins or financial debts. The word Jesus uses in Matthew 6:12 is not the typical word for sin (*hamartia*), but is the word that typically refers to some sort of financial debt or burden (*opheilēma*). However, in the parallel version of Luke 11:4, Jesus does use the normal word for sin, but then switches to the same word for debt that Matthew uses. So is Jesus referring to sin or debts? The answer is both. Jesus is referring to anything that you might have against someone else, or which they might have against you, being either a fault committed or finances owed.

When you talk to God, ask Him for release from all your burdens, whether they are moral or financial. Again, if it is something weighing on your heart and mind, then it is fair game for your conversation with God. This might sound nice when it is directed toward you, but Jesus also invites you to release other people from the faults they have done to you or the finances they owe. This is much harder to talk to God about, and is not something that most people want to do.

By the way, it is worth mentioning that the word Jesus uses for "forgive" here (*aphesis*) does not mean to simply erase. There are two words for "forgiveness" in the Bible, and the one Jesus uses here means something closer to "release." Very often, there are conditions attached to this form of forgiveness, so that you will not experience it unless you first fulfill the conditions. (See the volume in this "Christian Questions" book series about forgiveness which explains this in more detail.) In this case, when you talk to God about being released from your addiction to sin or your burden of debt, He is not just going to wave a heavenly magic wand and do away with your addictions to sin or your burdens of debt. Instead, in communication with Him, you and He will come up with a plan of action to break free from sin and pay off your debt. The same can be true with how you interact with those who owe you money or who have wronged you.

So again, when you talk to God about these things, He does not just come into your life and erase your past and do away with your debts, as much as you might like Him to do that. He first invites you to consider how you might release other people who have wronged you, and then He provides input and advice so you can also be freed from your own sin and debt. There are no easy fixes here, but it is something that God wants to talk with you about, and walk with you through.

Do not lead us into temptation, but deliver us from the evil one

God doesn't actually lead anyone into temptation (Jas 1:13), so this phrase probably means something closer to "Help us resist temptation when it comes." At a more basic level, this is an invitation by Jesus for you to talk to God about your areas of struggle. Since God wants to talk to you about everything and anything, He definitely wants to talk to you about any areas in which you face temptation.

This might be awkward for you, because maybe you think that God is so holy He doesn't want to hear about your secret thoughts, hidden behaviors, and impure desires. But if that is what you think, you are wrong. One of the main reasons Jesus became human is because God wanted to show humans that He loves us so much, He will step right into our sinful condition with us so that He can love us there and lead us out of the mess we find ourselves in. So go ahead; talk to God about your sin. It is only when you invite God into your sin with you that He will be able to begin delivering you from it.

When I try to deal with temptation by myself, I almost always fail. But I experience the most victory over temptation when I swallow my pride and realize that God is not going to be offended by what I am struggling with. When tempted, I invite God into the temptation with me to talk to Him about it. I might say, "Hey God, do you see what I'm dealing with here? What do you think? Should I do it? I really, really want to, You know." Then we talk about it, the pros and cons of doing what I am tempted to do, and usually, He persuades me to resist.

Yet even when I fall to temptation, rather than wallow in guilt and shame for days on end (the way I used to), I try to immediately invite God back into the mess I've caused. I have a sheepish laugh with Him about it, saying, "God, look at this mess. What was I thinking? I don't know why I did that … again. And just like every time before, it wasn't as fun as I thought it would be." Then we discuss what happened to cause me to fall into the sin, and how I can avoid these temptations in the future.

Be aware, however, that once we invite God into the sinful areas of our life, He doesn't stop with the one area in which we asked Him for help. After He helps us sweep one room clean, He usually points to a locked closet and says, "Now what's in there? Anything you need help with?" God is in perpetual "spring cleaning" mode, and once He gets going, there is no stopping Him. Along with locked closets, He might find some cobwebs in the corner and trash which we shoved under our bed hoping He wouldn't find. But He will.

This is why talking to God about our sin is so dangerous. There might be certain sinful areas of our life that we are rather attached to. It becomes somewhat painful when God turns on the light in those dimly-lit rooms and cobweb-filled basements, and starts to open up dusty boxes to see what's inside. But if we listen to His input, get His advice, and talk to God as we go, the process will be more liberating than painful. And though God never gives up, He also is not too pushy, but gently leads to the next area He wants to clean.

THE DISCIPLE'S PRAYER IS DANGEROUS

So the Disciple's Prayer can be quite dangerous. Later in this book we will consider ten dangerous prayers (see Chapter 5), but as we have seen here, the prayer that Jesus instructed His disciples to model is also full of life-changing and world-changing requests. So be careful about talking to God about the topics in this prayer. I am not saying you should not talk to God about them, but that you should be aware of the consequences that might come into your life as a result. Prayer is a power-ful gift from God, and every phrase in the Disciple's Prayer is a minefield just waiting to turn your life upside down ... but in a good way. Never forget that God is a loving Father who only wants what is best for His chil-dren. That means He only wants what is best for you. His plans for your life may seem scary at first, but they are always bigger and better than any plan you may have.

Imagine what your life would look like if you truly believed that God was your loving Father who only wanted what was best for your life, and so you sought to do everything possible to bring praise and glory to Him through your words and actions? What would your life look like if you sought after the Kingdom of God rather than the kingdoms of men? How would you function if you only had enough for today, and didn't know how God would provide for tomorrow? What might happen in your life if you worked to release people from their bondage to sin and debt as God works to release you from the same things? How might your life be different if you truly saw sin the way God sees it and didn't engage in the pet sins we think we cannot live without? Yes, this prayer that Jesus instructs His disciples to pray is revolutionary, life-changing, and dangerous.

Now although this is the prayer that Jesus taught His disciples to pray, it is not the only way to pray. We see this by comparing the "Disciple's Prayer" with the way Jesus Himself prayed in John 17. Though there are many similarities, there are also significant differences. This is what we will see in the next chapter, where we consider the true "Lord's Prayer."

CHAPTER 3

HOW DID JESUS PRAY?

There are numerous instances in the Gospel accounts of Jesus praying. Sometimes He prayed all night (Luke 6:12), though He also got up early to pray (Mark 1:35). Sometimes His prayers were long; sometimes they were short (John 12:28). What we can learn from this is that even with Jesus, there was no set way to pray. For Jesus, it seems that prayer was not so much a time that He set aside to specifically talk with God, but was closer to just picking up with an ongoing conversation with God.

The same can be true with you. If you always have the lines of communication open with God, then there really is no such thing as a long or short prayer, but just re-engaging with God in a conversation that has been going on for some time. This is why special postures or places for prayer, while occasionally helpful, can also be detrimental to your prayer life. The same goes for saying "Amen" at the end of your prayer. I still say "Amen" when I pray publicly, but this is just to indicate to others that I am now talking directly to them instead of to God. But if prayer is an ongoing conversation with

God, then it never really stops. You might temporarily stop talking about one particular issue or request, but the line of communication with God remains open and active, ready to be picked up at any time. This is partly what Paul meant when he wrote about praying without ceasing (1 Thess 5:16).

This is also how Jesus prayed. As you look at the various prayers of Jesus in the Gospels, it becomes obvious that the prayer life of Jesus was simply part of an ongoing conversation He had with God. He was always aware of God's presence, and always kept focused on what God was doing through Him and around Him, and when Jesus sought to have a direct conversation with God, it was not as though He started and stopped His prayers, but rather just picked up where He left off before, or turned to God (who was already there) and simply started talking to Him about what was currently going on. Similarly, the "end" of the prayer is not the end of praying, but just a temporary lapse or pause in the discussion that would be picked up again at a later time.

Let us look at the true Lord's Prayer in John 17 to see this in more detail, and also to learn what we can from how Jesus prayed.

THE LORD'S PRAYER

John 17 records the prayer that Jesus prayed in the Upper Room with His disciples at the conclusion of their last supper together. Though the Gospels frequently record Jesus going off by Himself to pray, this is the only recorded prayer of Jesus of any length which provides an indication of the sort of things Jesus might have said when He prayed. So if you want to learn how to pray like Jesus, there is no better prayer in Scripture to study. In the sections below, you will see how Jesus structured His prayer, the posture He used, His prayer requests, and also a few insights into how Jesus did *not* pray. It is important to note that even though these provide insights into how Jesus prayed, this does not mean that you must follow the exact same structure, outline, or posture, or even that you should pray for the same things that Jesus prayed for. This prayer in Scripture is not provided so that we might copy it, but so that we might learn more about the heart of Jesus and how He communicated with God.

The Structure of the Prayer

The prayer is divided into three basic sections. First, Jesus prays for Himself (17:1-5), then for His disciples (17:6-19), and finally for all who would believe in Him (17:20-26). The prayer of Jesus has a "concentric circle" approach to ministry, where Jesus' relationship with God is at the center, and Jesus works His way out from there to the disciples and then to all who will believe in Jesus, which includes us today. While not all prayers must follow this pattern or structure, it is nevertheless helpful to note that Jesus does begin by praying for Himself and His relationship with God.

If you are like most people, you have found that it is nearly impossible to pray if you are not in right fellowship with God. After all, if you are not on "speaking terms" with God, how do you expect to speak with Him? So although this prayer of Jesus does not provide a universal pattern for all prayer at all times, it is nevertheless helpful to remember that since prayer is a conversation with God, it is important to make sure that you are in a good relationship with God. How can you talk to Him if you don't want to be near Him or with Him?

So while on the one hand, you must make sure that your prayers are not self-centered and that you only pray for yourself and your needs, it is nevertheless true that the starting place for prayer is your own relationship with God. When sin, disobedience, or rebellion get in the way of your communication with God, your prayers should include some confession and repentance. Even when your relationship with God is wonderful, it is still a good idea to include some relationship building conversation in your prayers.

Again, never forget that prayer is just like communicating with anyone else, such as a spouse or friend. In any relationship, it is wise to frequently check the pulse of the relationship, and take care of any issues that are between you so that the friendship and communication can continue. If you would do this with a friend, spouse, or coworker, how much more should you do this with God?

The Posture of Prayer

If you have ever seen an artistic rendering of what Jesus looked like during His prayers (such as the prayer in the Garden of Gethsemane in Matt 26:36-56), you will likely remember that the portraits depict Jesus as kneeling before a rock, with this hands clasped in front of Him on the rock, and His eyes turned upward toward the sky. As a result of pictures like this, some believe that this is the proper posture of prayer.

Yet note that nothing much is said in John 17 (or anywhere else, for that matter), about the posture of Jesus during His prayers. The text does not tell us if Jesus was sitting, standing, or reclining. Since Jesus and His disciples are still indoors at this point, and since reclining on the floor was the typical way of eating meals in first century Middle Eastern culture, it is possible that Jesus was still on the floor while praying. Or maybe He stood up. We just don't know. One thing is for sure though: Jesus definitely was not folding His hands, bowing His head, and closing His eyes. To the contrary, the text says He "lifted up His eyes to heaven" (17:1), which indicates that His eyes were open and His head was raised.

But even this posture is not the "God-approved" posture for prayer. It is not as if such things as kneeling or standing, arms up or arms down, eyes open or eyes closed make any difference in whether or not God hears and answers our prayers. If God is concerned about any sort of posture in our prayers, it is the posture of our hearts, which no one can see but Him alone. So when you pray, don't be overly concerned about what your hands, your head, or your eyelids are doing. The only thing that matters to God is what is going on in your heart. As long as you are having a conversation with Him, your hands can be busy at work and your eyes can be alertly watching your surroundings (I often pray while I drive).

Just like with any other conversation with any other person, there is no "one right way" to sit or stand. The posture of prayer has nothing to do with who you are talking to, but everything to do with what the two of you are doing while you talk. God is happy to talk with you wherever you are and whatever you are doing. So whether you are vacuuming, driving, mowing the lawn, walking the dog, performing your duties at work, watching TV, laying on your bed, or reading this book, you can be in conversation with God.

The Prayer Requests

The previous chapter looked at the "Disciple's Prayer" and some of the things you can pray for when you communicate with God. Here in the "Lord's Prayer," we see that Jesus prayed for some of these same things. For example, Jesus prayed that God's name would be glorified through His own life and ministry (17:1-5). In praying for His disciples that they would carry on the work that Jesus started (17:16-19), Jesus was essentially praying that the Kingdom of God, or the rule and reign of God, would continue to spread upon the earth. He does not pray for daily sustenance or the forgiveness of debts, but He does ask that God protect His disciples from the evil one (17:11, 15).

One of the main requests in Jesus' prayer is that those who believe in Him will live in unity with each other, just as Jesus lives in unity with God (17:11, 21, 23). I find it sadly ironic that although this is the primary prayer request of Jesus for His church, the one thing that the church is most known for is our lack of unity. When the world thinks of Christians, they often think of people who are divided. And they are not wrong. There are thousands of denominations in the world, and we are all divided over some of the silliest things. Yes, some of the divisions are necessary and important, like whether or not Jesus was truly God, but when we divide over the mode of baptism, whether women can be pastors, music styles, or church governance structure, such divisions bring great sadness to Jesus. In reality, there are relatively few things we must all agree on. A few such items might be that eternal life is by faith alone in Jesus Christ, that Jesus is the Lord and Master of the church, and that we are to love all people in His name. Beyond these, there should be nothing that divides us.

I sometimes think that if the church truly wants to rise up and bring glory to God as Jesus prays here in John 17, the best thing we could do is to stop praying for Aunt Mabel's bunion, our neighbor's lost dog, and how the rent is overdue, and instead seek to create unity in the church as an answer to Jesus' prayer. This is not to say that you cannot talk to God about health issues, lost pets, and financial difficulties. You can and you should. Since God loves you, He wants to hear about such things. But at the same time, do not allow these relatively minor issues to cloud your vision for the unity that Jesus prayed for. In your prayer life and daily life, work to develop a broader vision for prayer than how we can use it to tell God about our aches, pains, and bills. Work toward what Jesus worked for, which is to glorify God through carrying out His will on earth, which is primarily accomplished through living with one another in love and unity. When you pray for this, you can know with certainty that you are praying according to the will of God.

JESUS CONVERSED WITH GOD

As you read through the prayer of Jesus, the one thing you might notice is that it is very conversational. Though there are some patterns and requests which align with the "Disciple's Prayer" from Matthew 6, Jesus also departs from that model prayer, and simply talks with God about what is on His heart. Since Jesus knows that He is about to be arrested and crucified, His concern is that God's work on earth will be continued, that His disciples will be cared for and protected, and that all who come to follow Jesus will be part of God's unified plan for the work He is doing in the world. And since these issues are on the mind of Jesus, this is what Jesus talks to God about.

Notice that Jesus does not engage in needless repetition of the name of God. Nor does He try to ward off the devil. Jesus is not concerned with including any flowery or fancy language to impress those who are present with His advanced holiness. Truthfully, if you compare the prayer of Jesus in John 17 with any of the other passages in John where Jesus is talking to humans, there is almost nothing that sets this prayer apart from any other conversation. The conversation Jesus has with God sounds pretty much just like a conversation He might have with Peter, or Matthew, or John. For Jesus, communicating with God was just like communicating with others.

Note as well that this prayer seems to be a continuation of a much longer conversation Jesus has been having with God. Because this prayer is part of a longer, ongoing conversation, Jesus does not have the need to fit everything in, follow a prayer outline, remember any prayer requests, or even begin and end the prayer with a flowery introduction and conclusion. In fact, between

John 16:33 where Jesus stops talking to His disciples and John 17:2 where He starts talking to God, the only real transition is that Jesus looks heavenward. It is so casual, it is as if Jesus had been talking to the disciples and then turned His head to start talking to God. His tone and language and posture and even the content of what He is saying does not really change. For Jesus, prayer is just continuing a conversation with God.

When understood this way, prayer becomes much less of a mystery about how to pray, what to pray for, who can pray, or where to pray, and much more like a conversation you have in everyday life. If you can talk with a friend, you can talk to God. This is how Jesus prayed, and how you can pray too.

CHAPTER 4

HOW TO RECEIVE ANSWERS TO PRAYER

Earlier in this book I said that prayer is nothing special. Though this is true in a sense, it is not so true in another sense. Prayer may be the most special thing ever. Think about it. Prayer gets you face time with God. Prayer is one-on-one with the creator of the universe. Most amazingly, prayer allows you to give your input into what God is doing in the world. Through prayer, you get some say in how God runs the universe. Imagine that! Furthermore, I am convinced that there may be some things which God wants to do in the world, but He won't do except through prayer. That is, there are aspects of God's will which are contingent upon people asking Him for them. There are some things God won't do unless people ask Him to do it.

Yet if this is so, why is it that so many of our prayers go unanswered? Yes, I know that there is no such thing as an unanswered prayer. I know that God saying "No," is just as much of an answer as God saying "Yes." So maybe a better way of asking the question is, "Why does prayer seem so ineffective?" If prayer gets you face time with God, if prayer grants you some say in how God runs the universe, then why does it seem that most of your prayers don't actually affect much change?

If this is your frustration with prayer, there are three basic answers for you to consider. First, maybe you are not praying according to the will of God, or what it means to pray in Jesus' name. Second, maybe you don't understand how prayer works. Finally, maybe you don't quite understand how to receive answers to your prayers. This chapter provides input on these three areas.

PRAY ACCORDING TO THE WILL OF GOD

One of the benefits to approaching prayer as a conversation with God is that prayer no longer becomes a way to get stuff from God, but instead becomes primarily a way to grow in your relationship with God. When prayer is an ongoing conversation with God, you learn that prayer is not about presenting your wish list to a Santa Claus in the sky, but is instead about getting to know the heart, desires, and goals of a person who loves you very much.

As you get to know the heart, desires, and goals of God for your life and for this world, you come to better understand the sorts of things God wants you to ask Him for. And when you ask for the things that God wants you to ask Him for, He will always say "Yes," because these requests are according to His will. So the key to seeing God answer your prayers is to learn what is important to God and what He wants to accomplish in this world, and then pray for those things.

As you do this, you will also discover that the things God wants are also the things you want. Though you may think you want a mansion with a fancy car, when you grow in your relationship with God, you discover that such material possessions are not what your heart really longs for. Your heart actually longs for the things God longs for. God wants you to live in fellowship and unity with Him and with others, and be at peace with all people. God wants you to be generous, kind, gracious, patient, and merciful, just as He is with you. So when you ask God to help build these things into your life, He is more than happy to bring them to pass.

When Psalm 37:4 says that if you delight in the Lord, He will give you the desires of your heart, this does not mean that God will give you whatever it is you want. It means that when you enjoy being in God's presence, and when you enjoy talking with God and learning about what is important to Him, He places His desires into your own heart, so that your desires come from His desires. He gives you the right things to desire, and then He works to help fulfill those desires. This is what it means to ask according to the will of God (1 John 5:14).

Praying according to God's will then, is not so much when we ask God for the things we want, but when we first seek God's heart and will on various matters, and then ask Him for these things. Proper prayer occurs when we speak God's heart back to Him, asking how we can get actively involved in what He is already doing in the world. Prayer is when we verbalize to God our desire to join Him in accomplishing His will that He has whispered to our hearts.

PRAY IN JESUS' NAME

A similar concept to praying according to the will of God is praying in Jesus' name. Many people seem to think that to "pray in Jesus' name" simply means to tack the words "… in Jesus' name, Amen" at the end of their prayer. This is not what it means at all. To pray "in Jesus' name" means to pray as if Jesus Himself was praying our prayers.

When an ambassador visits another country "in the name of the king" (or president), it is as if his king (or president) is speaking the words that the ambassador speaks. The leaders of these other countries are to assume that whatever the ambassador says, it is as if the king (or president) himself said them. The ambassador speaks "in the name of the king."

Since this is so, the ambassador must be certain that what he says is exactly what the king himself would say.

If an ambassador says something foolish or insulting, he could easily start a war, ruin a trade agreement, or destroy a treaty. To be a good ambassador, the ambassador needs to know the mind and heart and will of his king so intimately that the two minds are nearly one.

This is what it means to pray "in Jesus' name." These three words are not a magical incantation that you can tack on to the end of your prayers to get whatever you want. Instead, to pray in Jesus' name means to develop a mind frame in which you know you are speaking for Jesus. You are approaching the throne of God as if Jesus Himself was speaking through you. This means that, like an ambassador, you must so intimately know the mind, heart, and will of Jesus in whatever situation you are praying about, that the words you speak are the same exact words Jesus would speak if He Himself were the one making the petition to God.

In John 14:13-14, Jesus instructs His disciples to pray in His name. His words can be expanded and paraphrased as follows:

> But when you pray, spend time thinking about what I value, what I instructed you to know, how I lived my life, the kind of example I provided, the people I hung out with, the goals I sought to achieve, and the relationship I have with God. Take careful notice of what I taught and what I prayed for. Then, offer your requests to God in light of these things. And when you do, make these requests boldly, knowing that the words you speak are the

same words I am speaking. When you pray this way, know that your prayers will be answered.

So when you are praying something which you know with absolute certainty is the will of God, and which Jesus Himself would pray, this is when you can pray "in Jesus' name," as if He Himself were praying your prayers. You can know you are praying according to the will of God when you pray the things Jesus prayed for, or when you pray for the things which God has revealed in Scripture.

But what about when you are not quite as certain? What about when you want to pray for something, but you are not sure whether or not your request is the will of God or your own will? Does this mean you cannot and should not pray for such things? No. You can and should. But rather than pray for such things "in Jesus' name," this is when it is best to tell God, "… yet not my will, but yours be done." In other words, tell God what is on your heart and mind, but also let Him know that you understand that you are unsure about His will in this situation, and although you have presented your requests to Him, you will submit to whatever He decides to do. Unless you are praying the clear commands and instructions of Scripture, it is likely that most of your prayers will be of this second sort, where you recognize that your heart can be deceived and your mind darkened, and so you leave the decision up to God.

So to pray in Jesus' name does not mean that you

will get whatever you ask for if you simply tack on some magic words at the end of your prayer. To receive what you ask for in prayer requires you to pray according to the things God wants you to pray for, or to pray for the things that Jesus Himself prays for. When you pray "in Jesus' name," this means that you should pray as if it is Jesus Himself praying through you. When you pray, if you cannot imagine Jesus praying for it, you probably shouldn't pray for it yourself. Can you imagine Jesus praying for a Lamborghini and a mansion? No? Then you shouldn't pray for such things either.

But when you do pray for the things Jesus would pray for, when you do pray for the things that are according to the will of God—and especially His revealed will in Scripture—this is when God steps in to act boldly and mightily in response to your prayers. This is why the prayers of a righteous person accomplish much (Jas 5:16). It is not because the person is so righteous and holy, but because such a person better understands the heart of God than others, and so when they pray, they are praying according to the will, desires, and goals of God. When you pray this way too, your prayers will also accomplish much.

HOW PRAYER WORKS

Another reason you sometimes don't see God working in response to your prayers is because you might not understand how prayer works. Or maybe it is better to say that you might not understand that prayer *is* work. This truth is something I learned from C. S. Lewis in his essays "Work and Prayer" in the book, *God in the Dock,* and "The Efficacy of Prayer" in the book, *The World's Last Night.*

Essentially, the argument of C. S. Lewis is that any responsibility in this world which God can pass on to human beings, He does pass on to human beings. He prefers not to do something if a human can do it. This is because we are His ambassadors on earth. As the image of God in this world, we carry out the work of God. Toward this end, God has provided two means by which we can accomplish these God-given tasks: work and prayer. And just as we view work as a way of getting things done in the world, we must begin to view prayer similarly.

Here are some excerpts from Lewis' essay, "Work and Prayer" which explain this point:

> Everyone who believes in God must therefore admit (quite apart from the question of prayer) that God has not chosen to write the whole history with His own hand. Most of the events that go on in the universe are indeed out of our control, but not all. It is like a play in which the scene and the general outline of the story is fixed by the author, but certain minor details are left for the actors to improvise. It may be a mystery why He should have allowed us to cause real events at all, but it is

no odder that He should allow us to cause them by praying than by any other method.

Pascal says that God "instituted prayer in order to allow His creatures the dignity of causality." It would perhaps be truer to say that He invented both prayer and physical action for that purpose. He gave us small creatures the dignity of being able to contribute to the course of events in two different ways. He made the matter of the universe such that we can (in those limits) do things to it; that is why we can wash our own hands and feed or murder our fellow creatures. Similarly, He made His own plan or plot of history such that it admits a certain amount of free play and can be modified in response to our prayers. If it is foolish and impudent to ask for victory in war (on the ground that God might be expected to know best), it would be equally foolish and impudent to put on a [raincoat]—does not God know best whether you ought to be wet or dry?

The two methods by which we are allowed to produce events may be called work and prayer. Both are alike in this respect—that in both we try to produce a state of affairs which God has not (or at any rate not yet) seen fit to provide "on His own." And from this point of view the old maxim *laborare est orare* (work is prayer) takes on a new meaning. What we do when we weed a field is not quite different from what we do when we pray for a good harvest. But there is an important difference all the same.

You cannot be sure of a good harvest whatever you do to a field. But you can be sure that if you pull up one weed that one weed will no longer be there. You can be sure that if you drink more than a certain amount of alcohol you will ruin your health or that if you go on for a few centuries more wasting the resources of the planet on wars and luxuries you will shorten the life of the whole human race. The kind of causality we exercise by work is, so to speak, divinely guaranteed, and therefore ruthless. By it we are free to do ourselves as much harm as we please. But the kind which we exercise by prayer is not like that; God has left Himself discretionary power. Had He not done so, prayer would be an activity too dangerous for man and should have the horrible state of things envisaged by Juvenal: "Enormous prayers which Heaven in anger grants."

Prayers are not always—in the crude, factual sense of the word—"granted." This is not because prayer is a weaker kind of causality, but because it is a stronger kind. When it "works" at all it works unlimited by space and time. That is why God has retained a discretionary power of granting or refusing it; except on that condition prayer would destroy us. It is not unreasonable for a headmaster to say, "Such and such things you may do according to the fixed rules of this school. But such and such other things are too dangerous to be left to general rules. If you want to do them you must come and make a request and talk over the whole matter with me in my study. And then—we'll see."

I love how Lewis concludes his essay by talking about prayer as if it were a conversation you had with a headmaster of a school in his study. This is right in line with what we have been learning in this book about prayer. More importantly, though, Lewis shows the close connection between work and prayer as a means of accomplishing God's will in the world. This explanation by Lewis shows how important prayer is, and also how to go about accomplishing God's will in this world.

Prayer is not a lesser form of work, but a greater and more powerful form. This is why God leaves Himself some discretionary power to say "No." God is willing to talk to you about everything and anything, but since He alone knows everything, He allows Himself the freedom to say "No" to the things you ask for which run contrary to His will, goals, and purposes for this world. This understanding of prayer as a form of work brings us to the third truth which will help you understand how God answers your prayers.

HOW GOD ANSWERS PRAYER

One of the primary ways God wants to answer your prayers is to have you answer them yourself. As you grow in your relationship with God through prayer, God places His desires into your heart so that you know how to pray according to His will. But God doesn't just place His desires into your heart so that you can pray for them. No, God gives you these desires so that you can actually go do something about them. Very often, the burdens God places on your heart and mind regarding the needs or issues of other people is not simply so that you can pray about them, but so that you can do something about them.

It is not uncommon in the church, and especially in church prayer meetings, for people to gather together and share the prayer requests that lay heavy on their hearts. Then, after they share these requests, they sit in a circle and pray about them. They might pray for the neighbor lady whose husband is in the hospital, for the coworker who just got laid off, for the homeless people to find work, and for more people to start showing up for church. These are all valid prayer requests, and all of them, I believe, are within the will of God. However, I do not believe that God wants us to do nothing but pray about these requests. I think God sometimes makes needs known to us, not so that we can pray about them, but so that we can do something about them.

I once saw a comic strip where a guy was praying, and he said, "God, why aren't you answering any of my prayers?" God's reply was, "I was about to ask you the same thing." Praying for needs is important, but one way God wants to answer our prayers is by us going out to be the answer to our own prayers. Sometimes we fail to see answers to prayers, not because God doesn't care or doesn't want to answer, but because God is saying to us, "Answer your own prayer! Why do you think I laid that burden on your heart?" He lays needs upon our minds so that we can both pray and do something about these needs.

Proper petitionary prayer is when we speak God's heart back to Him, asking how we can get actively involved in what He is already doing in our lives and in the world. Prayer requests are not primarily those petitions we present to God, but are instead the verbal requests we make to Him which mirror the requests He has whispered to our own hearts. In a sense, we could almost say that God prays to us so that we can pray His prayers back to Him. God lays on our hearts and minds the things He wants done in the world, and then as we become aware of these issues and needs, we pray these requests to God, asking how we can collaborate with Him in the work He is doing.

This is exactly the point of James 2. For centuries, the church has argued about James 2:14-26 and what it teaches regarding the connection between faith and works. This is tragic, for such a debate only shows that those who engage in it don't understand what James is talking about at all. The passage is not about how to determine whether or not our faith is genuine. The passage is about how to see God work in response to our faith. We could say that James 2 is about how to see God work in response to our prayers.

In the church that James was writing to, there was one group of people who had need of food and daily clothes. There were others within the church who could meet those needs by providing food and clothes. But rather than providing for the needs of others, this second group instead said to the first, "I have faith that God will provide for you." In modern church lingo, we say, "I'll pray for you."

James blasts this sort of thinking. He says, "What good is that? Faith isn't going to help in this situation! Faith isn't going to put food on their table or clothes on their backs! The reason God made those needs known to you is because you have the means to help. Don't believe in God to provide for the needs of others; you provide for them. Don't ask God to give them food; you give them food. Don't pray for God to give them clothes; you give them some clothes."

The point of James is that while faith is wonderful and prayer is good, talking about your faith and how you will pray for God's provision is worthless when it comes to actually helping these other people. Yes, it is true that God can provide for their needs, but the way God wants to provide for their needs is through you! Faith is not sitting back and waiting for God to act while we do nothing. Faith is when we recognize that God is pointing out the needs to us because we have the means to meet the needs. While faith alone is genuine and good, faith alone does nothing to help those in need.

So yes, faith can exist by itself. But what's the point? Yes, you can pray for the needs of those around you, but if you do nothing to actually meet those needs, why pray? Faith, by itself, is worthless. Prayer alone accomplishes nothing. For faith to truly be energized, for faith to truly move mountains, for faith to accomplish much, you must join your faith with your actions, and seek to meet the needs for which you pray.

Though there are some things only God can do, there are many things that God cannot do except through us. Prayer is not so much us asking God to do things for us, but us asking how we can do things with Him. Most of the things you pray for can be accomplished by inviting God to work through you to meet the need you pray for, and then stepping out in faith to actually meet the need. We could say that God prays to us before we pray to Him, and so our prayers to Him are nothing more than a recognition of what He has been inviting us to do in this world. When we see a need and we pray for it, it is only because God has revealed that need to us and has invited us to get involved with Him in meeting it. In some sense then, when we wonder if God hears and answers our prayers, what we should really be wondering is if we hear and answer His.

When we pray, "Lord, reach our community with the gospel!" God says, "Yes! I want to send you to reach your community with the gospel. Are you ready to love and serve them like Jesus? Let's go!" When we pray, "Lord, help that homeless man find a job," God says, "Okay. I will do that if you take some time to go help him find a job." When we pray for God to end violence, stop wars, rescue victims, feed the hungry, clothe the poor, and help the sick, God is asking us to do the same things with Him. Indeed, God cannot do these things unless we participate with Him. Sometimes prayer is not so much a question of whether God hears our prayers, but whether we hear His.

As a pastor, I participated in the Wednesday night prayer meetings of our church. One week, one of the elders shared a prayer request about a retired pastor who was moving into town the following Wednesday. He asked that we pray for this man's transition, that he would safely arrive in town and get unpacked and settled in without problems. So the next Wednesday, when everybody gathered for our weekly prayer meeting, I began by announcing that God had heard our prayer and answered. I said that a whole group of people from the church had shown up to help this retired pastor unpack his moving van and get settled into his new house with his wife. The people were ecstatic to hear that God had answered our prayer in such a tangible way and that He did so through some of the people in our own church. Then they asked who these people were, for none of them had heard that this was happening. I smiled and said, "It's us. Let's go." And we went. There was some grumbling later on that the pastor had cancelled the prayer meeting to go move boxes, but overall, I think people got the point.

I hope you do too. If you want to see God answer your prayers, the first place to look for answers might be in your very own life. God does want to answer your prayers, and He probably wants to answer them through you.

CHAPTER 5

10 DANGEROUS PRAYERS

Although prayer is simply talking to God as you would talk to a friend, prayer is not something to take lightly. As indicated previously in this book, through prayer, God gives His children divine "say so." Prayer gives us a seat at God's council table, where He hears our input and bases some of His decisions on what we say. For this reason, prayer can be quite dangerous. But this is also why God sometimes answers our prayers with a "No." Ultimately, as C. S. Lewis pointed out, God gives Himself discretion on whether or not to grant our requests, because without this discretion, the power of prayer would destroy us.

Nevertheless, in my experience, there are some prayers that God always grants, and these prayers are quite dangerous to you and to your life. The reason God always grants these prayer requests is because they are within His will for our lives. In praying them, however, we often fail to realize how devastating these requests will be to our lives once they are granted. So in this chapter I want to share with you the ten most dangerous prayers you can pray. Although these prayers are dangerous, I still recommend that you pray them, for while they may seem to destroy your life at first, they will ultimately allow you to partner with God in extraordinary ways.

I share these dangerous prayer requests with you from personal experience. I have prayed all the dangerous prayers below ... and suffered the consequences as a result. But I reaped the rewards of these prayers as well. Though they ruined my life, they also saved my life.

I had my life all figured out, and it was all going according to my perfect plan. Then I started praying the prayers below, and before long, all my hopes and dreams lay shattered around my feet. I was publicly shamed and humiliated. I was without work and without money. I didn't know who I was or what I was supposed to do. I often tried to pick up the pieces of my life and glue them back together, but God would come through with His baseball bat and smash it all to hell (almost literally ... all of my plans and dreams deserved nothing more).

So I know the danger of these prayers, but also their importance and their power. When you pray these prayers, God will start to do work in your life as you never before imagined. Yes, it will be painful and scary, but God will take the pieces of your life and reconstruct them into a beautiful mosaic that reflects His light and love to a watching world. When you pray these prayers, watch out, for your life is about to change!

1. TEACH ME HUMILITY

After you pray this Christian prayer for humility, be ready for people to badmouth you, slander you, and drag your name through the mud. If you pray for humility, be ready for false accusations, for that "skeleton in the closet" to be revealed, or for people to belittle you and talk down to you as if you were inferior. Praying for humility is a dangerous prayer, because the only way to learn humility is to be placed in humbling situations. So if you pray for humility, be ready.

2. TEACH ME PATIENCE

Much like the prayer for humility, a prayer for patience is dangerous because the only way to learn patience is to be put in situations where your patience is tested and tried. If you pray for patience, you will soon be surrounded by the most annoying people you have ever met. Your car will break down when you are late for an appointment. Your children will go bonkers in the waiting room at the doctor's office. Your other prayers will go unanswered. When you pray for patience, get ready for setbacks, roadblocks, and pitfalls. So if you pray for patience, take a deep breath and hold on to your seat; you are in for a wild ride that will seem to last forever.

3. TEACH ME HOW TO FORGIVE

If you ask God to teach you how to forgive, He is going to do two things. He will first point out to you your many sins. He does this, not to shame you, but to show you how much you have been forgiven by God. We learn to forgive only when we come to understand how much we have been forgiven. After you have seen how much God has forgiven you, God will then bring people into your life who badmouth you, cheat you, sin against you, and do all kinds of horrible things to you. The only way to learn how to forgive others is to have people in your life whom you must forgive. So when you pray to learn how to forgive, watch out! For you are about to be hurt, slandered, maligned, mistreated, and abused. But when you finally learn the great ability to forgive, life will seem better, because you won't be bogged down with anger and bitterness.

As a side note, please note that forgiveness is not the same as forgetting. If you are being mistreated and abused, forgiveness does not require you to stay in that situation. Forgiveness does not require you to trust those who hurt and abused you. If you are being hurt, abused, or mistreated, you can forgive, but you must also get out. (I write more about this in my book on forgiveness in this Christian Question series.)

4. TEACH ME THE TRUTH

This prayer seems pretty innocent. What could be dangerous about truth? Don't we all want truth? Don't we want to know what God is really like, and what Scripture really says? Don't we want to know where we are wrong in our thinking and in our theology? The truth is that most Christians do not actually want to know where they are wrong. Most Christians don't *really* want to understand Scripture better. What they want is to have Scripture support their own beliefs and ideas. They want to remain safe and secure in their theological beliefs. They don't want to have their theological boat rocked.

This is why a prayer for truth is so dangerous. When you pray for truth, God is going to come into your life and start questioning some of your central beliefs about Him. The Holy Spirit will start raising dangerous questions about your understanding of certain biblical texts. Jesus will gently nudge you to rethink how you follow Him into the world. When you pray for truth, you will soon discover that some of your most cherished doctrines might be wrong. You may soon discover that the God you worship might not actually be the God revealed in Scripture. You may find that the way you are comfortable "doing church" is not actually found in the Bible.

When these sorts of truth bombs explode in your

life, it feels like the bottom has fallen away. It feels like there is nothing firm to stand on, that you have nothing left but questions and doubts. It feels like you are tumbling down the theological rabbit hole. For a time, you will not know up from down, in from out, or even right from wrong. Such theological vertigo is extremely disconcerting for most people, but it is what often happens when you pray for God to help you better understand Scripture and to show you where you are wrong in your thinking about Him and His ways.

The prayer for truth is a dangerous prayer. If you are comfortable in your theology and believe you are right in almost everything you believe about God and the Bible, do not pray this dangerous prayer. But if you do pray this prayer and are willing to see it through, the world God opens to you is one you will never want to leave. You will discover such freedom in thinking for yourself. When your eyes are opened to the truth, you will love how clearly you see things and will never want to return to the way you viewed things before.

5. LEAD ME WHEREVER YOU WANT ME TO GO

One way this Christian prayer is often prayed is with the words, "Here I am, Lord, send me." If you are like me, when you have prayed this prayer, you imagine that God is going to send you into a high-profile ministry with a big church and lots of prominence in the community. You imagine that maybe you will become an advisor to the President, or the CEO of an international Christian relief organization. And to hear many Christian leaders talk, this "upward ministry trend" does indeed seem to be the way God leads many people. This is why you will almost never hear Christian leaders say that God is leading them downward into insignificance and poverty. No, when most Christian leaders talk about how they were led by God, it is almost always to bigger churches, with more prominent ministries, where there will be larger salaries, and greater power.

While I do not deny that God sometimes leads people in these directions, I think that more often than not, when we follow Jesus wherever He leads, He actually leads us downward, but we refuse to go. Jesus leads us to the gutter. He leads us to the gates of hell. He leads us where lives are broken, where sin is blackest, and where Satan's chains are strongest. This is why the prayer to follow Jesus wherever He leads is so dangerous.

If you want to do great things for God in His Kingdom, you must understand that greatness in God's Kingdom does not look like greatness in the kingdoms of this world. It usually looks like the exact opposite. God's path to greatness usually does not mirror what you have in mind. God's path to greatness usually leads to prison, death, and the gates of hell. I once heard Francis Schaeffer say in an interview that if given the choice between two ministry positions, we should choose the one with less fame and glory, as this is likely where God is actually leading.

This dangerous prayer usually goes hand-in-hand with the prayer for humility. In my experience, choices in ministry usually come in pairs. There is often one path that leads to greatness and glory, and another path that leads to obscurity and insignificance. Though the temptation is to choose glory and honor, Jesus might actually be calling you to follow Him downward into humility. So be sure you really mean it when you tell Jesus you will follow Him wherever He leads.

But then sit back and enjoy the ride, for there is nothing as wonderful as being right where God wants you to be. You will start using your God-given gifts and talents in ways that are exhilarating and liberating. You will discover that you no longer feel like an outsider who is looking in to where all the action is taking place, but will instead find yourself in the middle of the action of God's expanding Kingdom work in this world. The joy of working with God in this world while using your gifts to expand the Kingdom is the most indescribable experience you can have in this life.

6. HELP ME UNDERSTAND THE PLIGHT OF THE POOR

The poor and the needy are all around us, and since Scripture so often invites us to consider the plight of the poor, it is normal and natural to pray for God to help you understand their situation, and to do what you can to help. But this is also a dangerous prayer.

One way God might help you understand the poor is by causing you to become poor yourself. Or maybe you will lose your job and struggle to find a new one. Until you have faced the difficulty of putting food on the table, of finding work to provide for your family, or of putting a roof over one's head, you cannot understand the plight of the poor. So if you like your nice house, your two cars, your steak dinners, and your Caribbean vacations, don't ask God to help you understand the plight of the poor. If you long to have compassion for others and empathy to understand the plight of the poor so that you can better help and care for them, this is the prayer for you.

7. MAKE ME MORE LIKE JESUS

Praying to be more like Jesus is a very common prayer in Christianity, yet I advise you to think twice the next time you pray this prayer. Jesus was beaten and bruised, scorned and mocked, despised and rejected. Are you sure you really want to be like Jesus? It's good if you want to be like Jesus in His abilities to teach, love, serve, and heal, but these abilities also led Jesus to be crucified and killed. I do not think it is possible in this world to have one without the other.

When you pray to be like Jesus, other people will do everything they can to stop you. And I'm not talking about the world. People of the world were actually quite open to Jesus. He was the friend to prostitutes, tax-collectors, and sinners. The main opposition to Jesus came from religious people. Similarly, when you seek to be more like Jesus, you will likely find that your pastor and your church-going friends might be the most upset. The reason is that Jesus often challenges the *status quo*, and especially the *status quo* that claims to represent God.

But when you pray to be more like Jesus, trouble will also come directly from God. God will always work to make you more like Jesus, and so when you invite Him to do this work in your life, He steps in and starts to break down, burn away, and slough off anything and everything that does not look like Jesus. God may purify your life with His refining fire, but it still burns.

Soon enough, however, you will have people saying that you are like a breath of fresh air to be around. People will sense the presence of Jesus in you, and will feel comfortable telling you things they cannot tell anyone else. They will desire to be with you and around you for reasons they cannot explain. People will feel loved and accepted in your presence, just as people felt accepted in the presence of Jesus. When we become more like Jesus, we allow others the joy of being themselves, free from judgment and open to God's love.

8. GIVE ME MORE FAITH

Christians like our beliefs in nice, neat packages. But life is not like that, and neither is life with God. When you pray for God to give you more faith, you are likely to enter into some of the most difficult and doubt-filled times of your life. You will begin to question everything you have ever known and everything you have ever believed. You may even begin to doubt God's goodness. You might begin to wonder if God even exists.

This is not bad. Embrace the doubts. Understand that if what you believe is true, it can stand up against all questions. Truth does not fear a challenge. There is no other way for your faith to grow unless your faith is tested, and faith is only tested by questions that challenge your faith. So don't be afraid of questions. Don't be afraid of doubt.

When you pray for faith, you will initially gain more questions than faith. But don't be alarmed. As you learn to live with doubt, God will make Himself known to you in new and exciting ways, and both your knowledge and your faith will grow.

9. GIVE ME VICTORY OVER SIN AND TEMPTATION

Praying for victory over sin is like praying for victory over a great enemy. It is wonderful to pray for, but how do you think this victory will be achieved? It will only be achieved by facing it in battle. David could have prayed all he wanted for victory over Goliath, but he never would have been victorious over Goliath if he had not faced the giant in battle.

It is the same with you and your sin. Yes, pray for victory over sin and temptation, but know that when you pray for this, the onslaught of sin and temptation will only get worse. The battle will intensify. The giants will come forth and will mock you and your puny sticks and stones with which you intend to do battle.

Just remember, of course, that when such temptations come in response to your prayer, God is not the one sending the temptation. God does not tempt; nor does He allow you to be tempted above what you can bear. So when you face your giant, or even a whole army of giants, do not fear, for God is on your side, and if you are facing heavy temptation, know that God is standing by your side ready to help no matter what your challenge might be. God will never abandon you in the fight, no matter how large the enemy.

So if you pray this Christian prayer, be ready for an onslaught of all the wiles of the devil, but also be ready for God to battle with you at your side. And as God battles at your side, you will become a better, stronger, and more able soldier in the ongoing fight.

10. PLEASE HELP MY ANNOYING NEIGHBOR OR COWORKER COME TO FAITH

This is a great Christian prayer. Does God want to reach your annoying neighbor or your rude coworker with the gospel? Of course He does! But in light of what you learned in the previous chapter, do you know how God is going to reach your annoying neighbor or coworker with the gospel? That's right. He's going to use you.

I once heard a story of a Bible study group who decided to make a prayer list of all the people they "disliked" the most, and then pray for these people every week as part of the Bible study. Over the course of the next ten years, all but one of the people on that list became believers. Furthermore, almost all of them became Christians because the members of that Bible study showed grace, love, mercy, and forgiveness to these "annoying" people in their lives.

If you are going to pray for someone, be prepared to answer your own prayers. When you pray for God to reach someone with the gospel, God is likely going to send you.

CONCLUSION

When you are going through difficult times in life, it is normal to ask, "Why me? Why is God allowing these things to happen to me?" When you are surrounded by devastation and difficulties and you find yourself asking, "What did I do to deserve this?" don't be surprised if the answer you receive back from God is, "You asked for it!" When you face difficulties in life, don't assume that God is punishing you, for the opposite is actually true. God does not punish.

Instead, when you face trials and troubles in life, it is more than likely that God is simply answering your prayers. God molds, forms, and shapes you in response to your prayers for Him to do so. But more often than not, in order for God to teach you humility or patience, to give you compassion for the poor, or to help you understand Him and His ways more clearly, He must first break you down so that He can then build you up and form you into what He wants you to be. The prayers suggested in this chapter will accomplish this reconstruction by God. These prayers are dangerous, but they are also essential, as we learn to follow Jesus wherever He leads.

CHAPTER 6

PRAYING POWERFUL PRAYERS

During the presidency of Lyndon B. Johnson, the Baptist minister Bill Moyers was asked to be the Presidential Cabinet's press secretary. At one of the meetings, President Johnson asked Bill Moyers to open the meeting with prayer. As Moyers began to pray, the President said, "Speak up, Bill, I can't hear you."

"I wasn't speaking to you, Mr. President," Moyers responded.

Imagine the audacity! And yet, this is exactly what we have been seeing in this book about prayer. Prayer is not fancy. Prayer is not for other people. Prayer is just talking to God. As we saw earlier in this book, prayer is when we "Jes' call 'im Father, an' ask 'im fer somethin'."

God doesn't need big words and long prayers. He doesn't need fancy or flowery language. He just wants us to come to Him as His child and talk to Him. That's the way all the saints in the Bible prayed. Every person in Scripture who is known for their great faith in God is also known for their simple and straightforward prayer life with God. Abraham, Moses, David, Elijah, Elisha, and Daniel were all men of great faith and simple prayers. It was also this way with Jesus.

And so it is not surprising that the prayers of the Apostle Paul are also simple and straightforward. Paul writes about prayer multiple times in his letter to the Ephesians (cf. Eph 1:15-21; 3:14-21; 6:18-20), but let us look at the description of his prayers in Ephesians 3:14-21 as an example of how Paul prayed and what he prayed for.

THE POSTURE OF PRAYER

For this reason I bow my knees ... (Eph 3:14a).

In Ephesians 3:14, Paul writes that when he prays, he bows his knees to God the Father. The term "bow my knees" is an idiom for kneeling. But does this mean that Paul knelt when he prayed? Maybe. But maybe not. While it might be true that Paul physically knelt on his knees when he prayed, Paul might also be using a figure of speech to describe the posture of his heart when he approached God in prayer.

The phrase "I bow the knees" comes from Isaiah 45:23. Isaiah 45 is a prophecy about the rule and reign of the Messiah. It is about how He alone will deliver Israel, and bring all her enemies to destruction. It is a lesson to the world in how He alone is Ruler and King. Isaiah writes that "Every knee will bow, every tongue confess" the Lordship of the Messiah (cf. Rom 11:4;

Php 2:10). Isaiah is saying that the Messiah deserves proper honor and respect, and that this can be symbolized by kneeling before Him. Yet even here, what matters more than the position of one's legs is the posture of one's heart. Despite what Paul writes here, one does not need to physically kneel in order to pray.

In fact, Paul himself might not have actually knelt when he prayed. Jewish prayers were often said while standing up (Matt 6:5). Jesus, of course, condemns the practice of praying in a way to be seen and heard by men, and so maybe Paul preferred to pray kneeling. But we just don't know. And that is exactly the point. God doesn't care about the position of your body as much as He cares about the posture of your heart. There is no "one right way" to position your body when you pray, just as there is no "one right way" to position your body when you talk to anybody else. Just as you can talk to anyone while you are doing anything, so also, you can talk to God while you are walking your dog, driving your car, mowing your lawn, doing the dishes, lying in your bed, or sitting on your back porch. Yes, you can even pray while kneeling, if you so desire. But regardless of your position, come with the respectful posture of a kneeling heart, submitting your life and your desires to God.

THE PERSON OF PRAYER

... to the Father of our Lord Jesus Christ (Eph 3:14b).

Note as well that, just like Jesus instructed, Paul directs his prayers to God the Father. He says he prays to the Father of our Lord Jesus Christ. Once again, this brings to mind the intimacy of prayer. It is like a little child coming to ask something from his daddy.

I read a story a while back about a man who was in the army who got promoted to the honorable rank of Brigadier General. When he received the news, he excitedly called his wife at home to inform her. But when she informed their young son, he became a little sad. When she asked the little boy why he was sad, he said, "Can I still call him daddy?"

Many people are like this little boy. They hear that the person to whom we pray is "God Almighty, Creator of Heaven and Earth, the Lord, Master, and Sovereign Ruler of the Universe," and while they are happy to pray to a God with such honorable titles, they are afraid to simply call Him "Father" and ask Him for something. But that is exactly what Paul does in Ephesians 3. He prays to the Father.

So while it is true that our Heavenly Father is King, Ruler, Judge, Lord, and Master, and therefore worthy of all honor and respect, it is also true that He is our Father, and wants us to simply address Him as such, coming before Him like a child to his daddy. I hear some people refer to God as Daddy or Abba, which is also fine. Again, the point is not to get too caught up with the right words, but to simply speak to God in a way that is comfortable and personable.

THE PETITIONS OF PRAYER

The most instructive elements about Paul's prayer in Ephesians 3:14-21 are his requests. By looking at what Paul prayed for, we can learn what sorts of petitions we can ask for in prayer as well. And the most striking thing about Paul's prayer requests is their audacity. Paul is not content to pray about toe bunions and the weather. He enters boldly before the throne of grace and tosses down the most daring requests. Paul does not pray for the mundane and commonplace; he prays for the impossible.

Do you ever get bored with prayer? If so, it might be because your prayers lack boldness. You know you're supposed to pray, but it sometimes seems that God doesn't hear or answer your prayers, or that you pray the same old thing over and over and over. When this happens, prayer becomes more of a habit you mindlessly perform than the powerful force in your life that it is supposed to be. But when you pray the way Paul prays, you will never get bored with prayer because you are asking for the impossible. When you pray the way Paul prays, your prayers will be anything but ordinary.

Paul prays for three things in his prayer. Clearly, these three petitions are not the only things Paul prays for when he prays (for he lists other prayer requests in Eph 1:15-21), but these three items provide some good ideas on what Paul prayed for and how you also can pray.

To Do What Cannot Be Done

That He would grant you, … to be strengthened with might through His Spirit in the inner man, … that you, being rooted and grounded in love (Eph 3:16-17).

The first impossible prayer request of Paul is that God will enable the Ephesian Christians to do what cannot be done. In Ephesians 3:16-17, Paul prays that God will give them the power … to be rooted and grounded in love. Initially, this may seem like just another ho-hum request from Paul. But when you read this request in the context of everything Paul has written in Ephesians 2–3, you see that one of the main problems in the Ephesian church was a failure to love each other.

Paul spent two chapters talking about how Jews and Gentiles are one in Jesus Christ, and how they are to get along. For some, this might seem like an impossible task. Some Gentiles would be thinking, "You mean I have to love that annoying Jewish neighbor of mine? There's no way! He's always judging me by his standards of living and acting 'holier than thou.' I can't love him. I can't fellowship with him!"

Some of the Jews, on the other hand, were likely thinking, "You mean I have to go over to that Gentile's house when he invites me over for dinner? I can't do that! He might serve meat sacrificed to idols! He might not be following the strict cleanliness laws. I might become ceremonially unclean! Paul can't be serious. There's no way I can get along with them!"

Many people today fail to grasp the deep divide that existed between Jews and Gentiles in Paul's day. If you were to take all the divisions that exist today—cultural, political, racial, economic, and religious—and lump them all together, this is similar to the strife that existed between Jews and Gentiles. And in Ephesians 2–3, Paul instructed them to get along and live in unity with each other. Here in Ephesians 3:17, he tells them that he is praying for them to be rooted and grounded in love for each other.

As I write this, every day includes news about how the world is being ripped apart by political divisions, racial strife, economic disparity, theological disagreement, and a wide variety of similar issues. The various political parties strongly disagree about critical issues such as healthcare, global climate change, gay rights, gun rights, open borders, and taxes. Regardless of where you stand on these issues, how easy will it be for you to love and befriend a person who holds opposite views? You might say, "There's no way. I can never be in the same room with such a person, let alone love and like them!"

Yet this is exactly what Paul is instructing the Ephesian Christians to do, and is exactly what he prays about in Ephesians 3:17. He wants people to love each other who, in every other walk of life, hate and despise each other. In other words, Paul is praying for the impossible. He is praying for two groups who hate each other to turn their hate into love.

Of course, the only way that Christians can do this is to understand that we are all loved by God, regardless of our political, economic, racial, social, cultural, or theological backgrounds. Once you see that God loves "them" as much as God loves you, you then begin to realize that He wants you to love "them" as well, regardless of whether or not they ever change their views. This is what Paul means then he talks about being "rooted and grounded" in love. We can only love others with the love of God when we know that we are loved and that the love of God which He extends unconditionally to us is also extended unconditionally to others.

So the first prayer request is an impossible prayer request. It is a request to do what cannot be done, to love those you would rather hate. Paul says, "I know you cannot love these people by your own power. So I am praying that God will give you His power to do what He asks, to love the unlovable." Do you want to spice up your prayer life? Start asking God to show you the people you hate, and then to transform your hate into love. Then step back and watch out, for you are about to encounter more Trump voters (or Hillary voters) than you ever knew existed. And it may not just be people with political or cultural differences, but people with theological differences as well. There are all sorts of issues that divide Christians, and Paul prays the impossible prayer for us to live with each other in love.

To Know What Cannot Be Known

> *That you ... may be able to comprehend with all the saints what is the width and length and depth and height—to know the love of Christ which passes knowledge (Eph 3:18-19a)*

Paul turns from praying for the Ephesian Christians to do what cannot be done, and asks God to let them know what cannot be known. The second prayer request in Ephesians 3:18-19 is a prayer for knowledge. Paul wants them to comprehend the width and length and depth and height of the love of Christ which passes knowledge. Once again, this is an impossible prayer.

Imagine a third grade teacher giving her class a test on quantum physics. They can't know quantum physics! Most educated adults can't grasp quantum physics. It would even be absurd to try to teach quantum physics to third graders. They don't have the right mathematical foundation or brain power to grasp even the elementary principles of quantum physics, let alone comprehend it.

This is similar to what Paul prays for here. He is praying that the Ephesian Christians would know the love of Christ, which passes knowledge. Paul prays for them to know what cannot be known. And unlike quantum physics which can be understood and grasped by some people, Paul's description of the love of Christ indicates that nobody fully understands or comprehends this vast subject. Paul writes about its width, length, depth, and height, indicating that the love of Christ is eternal, or infinite. It is without beginning or end. It cannot be measured or contained. It is wider than the universe, farther than the east is from the west, and deeper than the ocean. God's love is so vast, it cannot be understood or comprehended. Yet Paul prays that the Ephesian Christians will come to know it anyway.

This is another impossible prayer.

Nevertheless, it is a prayer which God works to answer. Though you will never come to fully understand, grasp, or comprehend the length, width, breadth, or height of God's love for you in Jesus Christ, you can come to learn a little more about it each and every day. This is what Paul hopes will happen with the Ephesian Christians, and which you can pray for yourself as well. Imagine how your life will change if each and every day you became more and more convinced of how much Jesus loves you? Imagine how much excitement each day would hold if you knew that somehow, in some way, Jesus was going to show you that He loves you.

Many Christians live with so much fear in their life. Fear of the future. Fear of the unknown. Fear of sickness and death. Fear of sin. Yet since perfect love casts out fear (1 John 4:18), as you come to know how much God loves you, your fear of all these things fades away as well. You come to know that you are safe and secure in the loving arms of God. You come to realize that even though you may face sickness, trial, danger, or sword, God will never leave you nor forsake you. If this sounds like what you want, then begin to pray for the impossible. Pray that you will come to know that which cannot be known. Pray that you will comprehend the love of Christ which surpasses knowledge.

To Be Filled With What You Cannot Be Filled

That you may be filled with all the fullness of God
(Eph 3:19b).

The third prayer request of Paul in Ephesians 3 follows the same pattern of the previous two. Paul continues to pray for the impossible. He prayed that the Ephesians would do what cannot be done and know what cannot be known. This third petition is that the Ephesian Christians would be filled with what they cannot be filled. The last half of Ephesians 3:19 contains Paul's prayer that the Ephesian Christians be filled with all the fullness of God.

How big is God? If you know some theology, you

know that God is omnipresent. This means that He is everywhere. God is fully present everywhere, and He even exists where nothing else exists beyond the limits of space and time. How great is God? How powerful is He? Again, in theological terms, He is omnipotent. He is all powerful. With a mere thought, He could obliterate the universe. With another mere thought, He could recreate it. He can do whatever He wants, wherever He wants, whenever He wants, however He wants. (Thank goodness He's a loving and merciful God—this kind of power would be terrible in the hands of a tyrant).

So with God's omnipresence and omnipotence in mind, think of what Paul is praying for in Ephesians 3:19. He prays that you, as a teeny, tiny speck of flesh and bones, made from dust, dying, decaying, sinful, insignificant piece of the vast universe, with life that is but a breath, that you may be filled with all the fullness of God. This is an impossible prayer request from Paul.

It wouldn't even matter if the structure of our body was much larger. When King Solomon built the first temple, he prayed a prayer on the day the temple was dedicated (cf. 1 Kings 8). He said, "But will God indeed dwell on the earth? Behold, heaven and the heaven of heavens cannot contain You. How much less this temple which I have built!" (1 Kings 8:27). Solomon, the wisest man who has ever lived saw the truth that God could not be contained in any sort of building or structure.

Yet Paul prays that the Ephesian Christians will be

filled with all the fullness of God. This also is an impossible prayer request. If God could not fill the temple, how can God fill a Christian? The solution, I believe, lies in how God answers the previous two impossible prayer requests from Paul. The fullness of God in the world is best seen in how Christians know they are infinitely and unconditionally loved by God and then learn to show this same love to others. The fullness of God in our lives is seen and experienced through the love that comes to us from God and the love that we show toward others. Just as Jesus is the fullness of God, we, as the body of Christ on earth, reveal the fullness of God to the world in the same way that Jesus did. We are filled with God the way Jesus was filled, as we show God's love to the world. So even this third and final impossible prayer request is answerable by God, and is answered as we show love to one another.

PRAYING IMPOSSIBLE PRAYERS

We have seen three impossible prayer requests from Paul. He prayed that the Ephesians would do what cannot be done, know what cannot be known, and be filled with what they cannot be filled.

Have you ever thought of praying for the impossible? How does your prayer life compare to Paul's? Paul prays for the impossible; what do you pray for? If your prayer life is boring, maybe it is because your prayer requests are boring. When you start praying for the impossible, you will quickly discover that prayer becomes exciting, thrilling, and even a bit terrifying. Rather than try to think up more things to pray about, you begin to wonder about the wisdom of praying for certain things. I mean, if you asked God to help you get along with that annoying neighbor, you might discover that God will start having you spend more time with that neighbor. Is that really what you want? If you pray for God to save the co-worker who intentionally blasphemes God when you're around, don't be surprised if you get assigned to work on a project with him. God wants you to ask Him to do the impossible, but only if you are willing to let Him do the impossible through you.

And when God starts to work in response to impossible prayers, He will do more than we can even ask or imagine. Paul writes in Ephesians 3:20 that God is able to do exceedingly abundantly above all we ask or imagine. What is impossible with men is possible with God. When we think something is impossible, God can run circles around it with His eyes closed and one hand tied behind His back. Nothing is impossible for Him.

So what is your impossible situation? Keep it in your mind and ask God to take care of it, knowing that He will likely take care of it through you. And don't worry about coming up with solutions for impossible problems. You don't have to make suggestions to God about how to handle impossible situations. All you have to do is present your requests to God and let Him take care of it. All you have to do is say, "God, here it is. I don't see a way out. It's yours." Ask God for the impossible.

CAN I GET AN "AMEN"?!

The last word of Paul's prayer in Ephesians 3 is the word "Amen." Based on this, as well as some other places in Scripture where the word "Amen" is used (cf. Deut 27:15-26; 1 Chr 16:36; Neh 5:13; 8:6), some Christians think that every prayer should be concluded with the word "Amen." But the word "Amen" actually means "Truly, so be it, let it be." When you pray impossible prayers, you are simply asking God to let it be as you have prayed. And when you pray according to His will, know that He will do what you have asked.

God does the impossible because this is how His name is glorified as stories of what God has done are shared from generation to generation. The story of Hannah in the book of 1 Samuel is a great example. Hannah was unable to have children, and so she prayed to God. She asked for the impossible. God heard her prayer and opened her womb, and within one year she gave birth to Samuel. We are still telling that story today.

Consider the account of Elijah in 1 Kings 18. He held a contest between God in heaven and the false god Baal. Elijah and the prophets of Baal built altars and each called on their own God to light the fire. God answered Elijah's prayer and rained down fire from heaven.

We could go on and on through Scripture. In response to Joshua's prayer, God halted the sun in the sky for a full day. In response to prayer, Peter was set free from prison. In a way, the Bible could be viewed as one long account of how God acts on behalf of those who pray impossible prayers.

And don't let the fact that they are Bible stories make you think that something similar could not happen with you. In November of 1835, George Mueller set out to prove that God hears and answers prayer. In looking for ways to prove this, he wrote:

> It needed to be something which could be seen, even by the natural eye. Now, if I, a poor man, simply by prayer and faith, obtained without asking any individual, the means for establishing and carrying on an Orphan-House, there would be something which, with the Lord's blessing, might be instrumental in strengthening the faith of the children of God, and being a testimony to the consciences of the unconverted, of the reality of the things of God. …When I was asking the petition, I was fully aware what I was doing. I was asking for something which I had no natural prospect of obtaining, but which was not too much for the Lord to grant.

By the time George Mueller died, the Orphan House founded and funded by prayer was able to house 1000 children at a time.

If you have spent much time praying for the impossible, you might have similar stories yourself. I once prayed a man out of a life-sentence in prison. From a judicial point of view, prison is probably where he belonged. But under mercy and grace, I was convinced that prison was not at all where God wanted him. So I prayed. On the night before his trial we went down to a local lake. It was March and the ice had just melted. He sat there on the shore, staring at the mountains thinking he would never see them again. Then he stripped off his shirt and pants and went swimming in the ice cold water, thinking he would never again feel lake water on his skin. The next day, he received a "Not Guilty" verdict. Why? Because of one thing—praying for the impossible. The man is now married, has a child or two, and is serving God with all his strength.

Does God answer prayers for the impossible? Of course He does. He is able to do exceedingly abundantly above all that you ask or imagine. If you want the impossible done in your life, pray for the impossible. Then let God work.

But what if you have prayed impossible prayers that were according to the will of God, and yet God never answered and never stepped in to work in impossible ways? What happens when you pray for God to work, but God doesn't seem to hear, listen, or respond? This question is considered in the next chapter.

CHAPTER 7

WHAT ABOUT UNANSWERED PRAYERS?

The most frustrating thing about prayer is how so many prayers seem to go unanswered. Yet many common Christian responses to unanswered prayer are less than helpful. When prayers go unanswered, it is never wise to quote Bible verses about needing more faith or that we should view our trials as an opportunity to prepare for even greater trials in the future. It is also unhelpful to spout the old Christian cliché that there is no such thing as unanswered prayer. We all know that sometimes God says "No" or "Wait" to our prayers, especially when we pray for things out of ignorance that might actually damage ourselves or others.

These sorts of responses to unanswered prayer are cruel and insensitive when said to the barren mother who prays for God to open her womb, the parents who pray fervently for God to heal a child with terminal cancer, the single person who is lonely and wants a spouse, or to the father who needs work so that he can feed and clothe his family. Are not all such requests within God's will? Of course they are! Are many of them impossible prayers? Yes! Then why does God seem to do nothing in response to such prayers?

The truth is that I don't really know. And neither does anyone else. So don't believe any pastor or theologian who says they do have the answer. Nevertheless, there are several things we do know about how God works through prayer and in our lives, and once we come to understand these truths, we begin to understand why there are so many unanswered prayers.

IT IS NOT A LACK OF FAITH

When we fail to see God respond to requests that we know are within His will, we must never think that the reason God did not respond positively is because we didn't have enough faith. Tragically, this is often what some Christians say and teach to others. "If you just had more faith," they tell the parents at a child's funeral, "God would have healed your child." This may be the most damaging lie ever told about prayer.

The reason many people say such things is because there are numerous passages in the Bible which seem to indicate that we must have "enough faith" before God answers our prayers (cf. Matt 13:58; 21:22; Mark 11:24; Luke 7:9, 50; 18:42; Jas 5:15-16). Yet the reason that modern Christianity has a twisted understanding of these passages is because we fail to grasp the nature of faith.

I teach a lot more about faith in my "Gospel Dictionary" online course, but briefly, it is critical to understand that faith does not come in "quantities." You cannot have 50% faith, or even 99% faith. Faith is more like a light switch that is either On or Off. Yet at the same time, faith is not an "all or nothing" proposition. That is, there are countless truths we can either believe or disbelieve, and they do not all stand or fall together. Some truths you will believe (the switch is On), and some truth you will not believe (the switch is Off). Some of these truths are hard to believe, while others are quite easy. Furthermore, you cannot choose to believe anything. You must be persuaded to believe, based on the evidence of facts which you already believe. Sometimes, when we come to believe something that we previously did not, this new belief has a cascading effect through numerous other beliefs—like a complex Excel spreadsheet. But they do not all stand or fall together like a house of cards.

When these truths about faith are taken into consideration, all of the passages from the New Testament about people's "lack of faith" take on entirely new meanings. It is not that people didn't quite have enough faith; it is that they simply didn't believe certain things. But even this truth about faith could be abused when talking to mothers who pray for sick children or fathers who pray for a job. So it is best to never question anybody's faith.

It is true that faith is a factor in our prayers. It is true that we must believe that God can do what we ask of Him. But faith as small as a mustard seed is able to move mountains (Matt 17:20). So the smallest amount of faith will do. Every person I have ever talked to or prayed with who has agonized in prayer over some desperate situation has more than enough faith for God.

Can we really believe that God is so petty that although He wants to heal a sick and dying child, He won't do so until the "faith meter" of the parents rises to a certain level? Does God sit idly by, watching our faith like a thermostat until it rises to 80%, but if we only get to 79%, He says, "Oh! So close! I'm going to have to let your child suffer and die." Is that what God is like? Of course not! This sort of god is a satanic lie.

So if the lack of "enough" faith is not the reason some prayers go unanswered by God, what is the reason? The answer is found in one of the things we humans value the most: our freedom.

IT IS A LOVE FOR FREEDOM

We humans love freedom. But we love freedom because God loves it more. Our love for freedom is a poor reflection of His love for freedom. And He doesn't just love His freedom, but ours. God wants us to have a relationship with Him, and created us for this very purpose. But in order for a true relationship to exist, there must be the freedom to reject that relationship. God desires that we love Him, but for love to be real, it must be free. And since He freely loves us, He gave us a degree of genuine freedom so that we might (or might not) love Him in return.[1]

This means that God is not in absolute control of all things. I know that this is a shocking thought to some, but it is the requirement for love. If God was in absolute control of all things, there could be no such thing as love, for love, by definition, does not seek to control.[2] On the one hand, if humans have a degree of freedom, but God forced His will upon people because He is stronger and more powerful, then this would not be love, but spiritual and psychological rape. On the other hand, if God did not give us a degree of freedom, and simply programmed us to do what He wants, then we would not be human, but would instead be robots, which cannot show genuine love. For love to truly be love, the object of love must be free to not love in return.

Since God does not control all things, but gives humans a degree of genuine freedom, this means that humans can use this freedom to do things that are contrary

[1] For an excellent discussion and defense of this idea, see Thomas Jay Oord, *The Uncontrolling Love of God* (Downers Grove, IL: IVP, 2015).
[2] Ibid., 181.

to God's will. In other words, we can sin. This explains why this world is full of sin. Sin happens because humans use our God-given freedom in a way that God does not want. And because freedom is genuinely free, God cannot simply take it back or turn it off when we seek to use our freedom in ways that are damaging and hurtful to ourselves and others.[3] Sinful human activity such as theft, rape, murder, and war are all contrary to God's will, but they happen because God provided freedom to humans, and some humans use this freedom in hurtful and harmful ways.

But it is not just sin. There are also natural disasters. Could not God stop natural disasters without violating anyone's free will? Well, the truth of the matter is that there are a nearly infinite number of factors that go into any single natural disaster, and a good many of these factors involve free human decisions.[4] Hurricanes and floods don't just come out of nowhere. Weather patterns, rain clouds, and rising sea levels are all influenced in various ways by the behaviors and actions of human beings. In a world where sinful or selfish actions have far-reaching effects, natural disasters cannot be magically averted if the forces of cause-and-effect are to remain in place.[5]

Due to creaturely freedom, many aspects of the

[3] Ibid., 168.

[4] Cf. the discussion in Gregory A. Boyd, *Satan and the Problem of Evil* (Downers Grove, IL: IVP, 2001), 218, and Gregory A. Boyd, *Is God to Blame?* (Downers Grove, IL: IVP, 2003).

[5] Oord, *Uncontrolling Love*, 175.

world are simply broken, and God cannot unilaterally fix everything that has gone wrong. While God does everything He can to protect us from the pain, there are some things God just cannot do without violating His gift of freedom, and therefore, violating love. As Greg Boyd writes:

> God's ultimate goal is to have creatures eternally participate in his triune love. The integrity with which he gives the risky gift of freedom is what makes this love possible and renders this freedom irrevocable. But this freedom is also what makes nightmares possible. God cannot avoid the possibility of these nightmares without also canceling out the possibility of love.[6]

However, this does not mean God is powerless or without resources to fix what is wrong with the world. Quite to the contrary, God's loving grace and wisdom are taking effect every day in our lives, and especially through our lives. As indicated earlier in this book, often when we pray to God to fix something that is wrong with the world, He agrees with our prayer and then asks us to fix it with Him.

It is for good reason that the New Testament speaks of the church as the "body of Christ." Just as Jesus was the incarnation of God on earth, the church is now the incarnation of God on earth. We are God's hands, feet, and mouth to a sick, lost, and hurting world, and there are many things that God wants to do in this world

[6] Boyd, *Satan and the Problem of Evil*, 215.

which He can only do in collaboration with us.

> God desires and needs human collaboration to accomplish his will. How can a struggling friend pay rent unless someone gives them money? How can racism be rooted out of the crevices of human hearts and minds unless someone teaches love and peace? How can child trafficking come to an end unless people stand up and rescue children? How can environmental pollution be reduced unless individuals and corporations take practical steps? The answer to all of these questions is, "They can't."[7]

Since God often works to answer prayer in collaboration with human partners, this means that answers to prayer often take time to appear. This is especially true when the answers to prayer require advances in the scientific fields of medicine, psychology, and sociology. Though many in these occupations do not recognize it, they are being guided by God to help the world go in the direction God desires.

But again, since God does not override human free will, such changes take time. And tragically, many people live (or have lived) in times when medicine has not yet solved the problem of cancer or barren wombs, when sociology and government have not solved the problem of homelessness and poverty, and when psychology has not yet solved the problem of mental illness or psychotic breakdowns. But God is at work, and all who wish to work with God in these areas should do as

[7] Karris, *Divine Echoes,* 147.

much as they are able to coordinate their work with God's work so that millions of prayers are answered.

So the reason many prayers do not get accomplished is not because they are outside of God's will, or even because God says "No" to them. To the contrary, He may very well be saying "Yes," but other factors and considerations are keeping His "Yes" from becoming a reality.

Sometimes these other factors include sin. Sometimes in order for God to say "Yes" to us, He would have to restrict or limit the freedom of someone else, which He is not always able to do. Sometimes God simply cannot do what we have asked, even though He would like to. Sometimes, God wants to do what we ask, but He wants to do it *with* us, and if we are unwilling to join Him in answering our own prayers, then God cannot do it on His own. Sometimes both we and God are doing everything possible to bring answers to our prayers to fruition, but a myriad of other factors keep it from occurring.

Nevertheless, when our prayers go unanswered, this is not the time to despair. We may not always know why certain prayers go unanswered, but we can know with certainty that unanswered prayers do not indicate a lack of care on the part of God. Even in unanswered prayer, God is there with us.

GOD STAYS AND PRAYS WITH US

When a woman prays for God to give her a child, God is right there with her, hugging and holding her, and crying with her about her emptiness. When a mother prays for her dying child to get healed, God is right there with her, grieving over a broken world where such things happen to innocent children. When a father cries out to God for employment, God is there providing input and advice to lead the man to a job.

Due to the problems that arise in this world of sickness and death, wombs do not always function the way God intended, medicine does not always work, and economies do not always provide work for all who need it. God is not a magician who can wave His magic wand to make everything better, but He is a Friend and Father who walks with us through the pain, stays with us in the darkest night, and leads us in the direction He wants us to go, even when things do not go the way He wants.

When your prayers go unanswered, know that this is not because God does not hear or does not want you to receive what you have asked of Him. Quite the opposite is true. When your prayers go unanswered, know that God is there with you in your pain and suffering, praying along with you for wisdom, insight, and direction, so that together, you might face and overcome all that this world throws your way. God will never leave you, forsake you, or abandon you. He will not withdraw from you to face the troubles of this world alone. When your prayers go unanswered, these are the times to turn toward Him for His care and prayer for you.

CHAPTER 8

OTHER QUESTIONS ABOUT PRAYER

I hope you have found this book helpful. If so, would you please leave a review on Amazon and tell others about the book as well? Thank you.

Nevertheless, you probably still have several questions about prayer. Since this is a short book on prayer, I imagine that not all of your questions were answered. Let me address a few of these possible questions here. If your question is not answered below, feel free to submit your questions about prayer (or any other subject), by joining my online discipleship group at RedeemingGod.com/join/. After you join, I will send you a few welcome emails and you can reply to any one of them to ask your question directly to me. You will also have the opportunity to take my online course on prayer (which is based on the content of this book) and receive further training about prayer by email. See you there!

CAN I PRAY WHEN I'M ANGRY AT GOD?

Many people wonder if they should pray to God when they are angry at Him. Life causes much pain and hardship in our lives, and these situations can create feelings of anger and resentment at God for not protecting us from them. Also, we sometimes feel that even though we try our hardest to serve and honor God with our lives, He does not do much to reward or recognize our efforts, and it is easy to feel neglected and overlooked. In such situations, we might become angry at God. When people get angry, they tend to turn away from God and stop praying

But this is exactly the wrong thing to do when you are angry at God. Rather than cease praying when we're angry, we should start praying even more, and then pray honestly to God, telling Him how angry we are and what we are angry about. In the experience of many, it is in our angry prayers where we often experience the greatest spiritual breakthrough with God. Why? Because it is only when we are angry that we finally let our guard down and tell God what is really going on in our hearts.

When we are not angry at God, we feel that we must hide our true emotions, thoughts, and feelings from God, and come to Him with pious words and "religious" language. But all such ideas disappear when we are angry. It is only when we are angry that we let go of our religious attempts to not "shock" God with our emotions of fear, frustration, confusion, and doubt. It is only when we are angry at God that we are honest enough with God to tell Him what we really think with words that really represent what is in our heart. God does not want us to be alone in our pain and anger. He prefers to be with us in whatever we face, especially if we think He is the one who caused it.

God loves your honesty and will often meet you there. It is often only in the angry prayer where the honest requests of our heart are revealed. God is not offended when we get angry at Him. He is not shocked or outraged when the frustrations of this life finally get the best of us and we lash out at Him with a burst of emotion, and even foul language. Instead, it is here, I am convinced, that God lets out a loving sigh and says, "Finally! I was wondering when you were going to tell Me what was *really* going on. I know what has been eating at you, but until you were ready to talk to Me about it, I wasn't going to force the issue. But now that we're talking ... well, I'm talking, and you're shouting ... we can finally start to communicate. So let it all out. Trust Me, I can take it. There is nothing you can say to Me that I haven't heard a million times before."

Remember, God is your friend, and He wants you to talk to Him like a friend. When you are angry at a good friend, you often shout it out with them, knowing that they will remain your friend no matter what you say. Honesty is always the best policy in friendship, even when it is honesty about anger and when the friend is God. So praying when you're angry might be one of the best times to talk to God.

In fact, yelling at God actually reveals your love for Him. When you go to God in your anger, it is usually because you know He can be trusted with your raw emotions. Therefore, going to God in anger is not a sign of hate, but love. Going to God when you are angry and frustrated is an indication of your love for Him, because you are taking your biggest problems to Him.

Children often get angry at their parents for not giving them something they really wanted (like candy before dinner), or taking something away that they had (like a sharp knife). The parents, if they are good parents, do this because the parent sees the bigger picture and knows what is best. So while no parent enjoys having their children upset at them in such situations, the good parent can handle the child's anger because they know they did what was best.

Similarly, since God is our Father, He sees the big picture and knows what is best for us. But like any children, we may get angry and upset at Him when life does not go as we hoped, dreamed, or planned. Often, genuinely bad things truly do happen, and if we think God is someone who always protects us from bad things, we might feel like He has betrayed us. But the worst thing we can do in such situations is fail to go to Him with our feelings of anger and betrayal. He wants us to come to Him and tell Him what we are thinking and feeling. Such feelings are not sinful or carnal, but come from ignorance about the situation or about the true nature and character of God. It is only when we come to God in honest anger that we keep the lines of dialogue open so He can start to reveal to us the truth about Himself and how life really works.

In other words, God would rather have you come to Him in anger than run from Him in anger. When you are angry at God but try to hide it, this doesn't please God, for this is just a form of pious dishonesty. Therefore, if you feel like yelling at God, don't hold back. Tell God what is wrong. Tell Him what you think. Lash out at Him in anger, for there is no tongue lashing that is worse than the actual lashing He already received on the cross. In both cases, He accepts the pain out of His great love for us.

Recently, one of my daughters was angry at me, and I couldn't figure out why. As I tried to figure out what had happened, I gently probed her with questions. But rather than answer my questions, she just kept saying "Nothing!" No matter what I asked, that was her answer. This is how we act toward God when we don't vent our anger at Him, and instead just clam up about what we're feeling.

So yelling at God is a healthy spiritual and relational practice. The Psalmists all understood this, and in the Psalms, we encounter some of the angriest writing in all of Scripture and much of it is directed at God. The Psalmists had raw emotions and were not afraid to vent at God. If you ever feel like yelling at God, read some of the Psalms and yell at God along with the Psalmists.

So are you angry at God? Are you angry about something He allowed to happen in your life? Go ahead. Yell at God. Curse if you have to. There is nothing you can say that God hasn't heard already… It's not like God has virgin ears. Tell God your blasphemous thoughts. You have permission to be honest with God about your thoughts and your feelings. God always prefers angry honesty over the sullen silent treatment. So yell away.

In my own experience, the times where I have heard God's voice the most clearly are the times when I have just finished lashing out at Him in visceral anger and outrage at how He failed me, my family, or this world. It is after I have used God as a punching bag that I feel His arms wrap around me and say, "Well done. I'm glad you finally got that out into the open. You've been hiding it away, and now that you've brought it out, we can talk about it. Oh, and by the way, before we do talk about it, I want you to know that I love you. Nothing you just said could ever get in the way of My love for you."

And then we talk.

WHAT ABOUT PRAYER FOR HEALING?

I believe God can and does heal. But we cannot demand healing, and more often than not, God does not heal without the help of doctors and modern medicine. The vast majority of "divine healing" occurs in coordination with the divinely-guided medical practices of our day.[1] This is, in fact, what James is referring to when he writes about the effectiveness of anointing oil for healing. There is no "magical" healing power to anointing oil. Instead, rubbing, or anointing, with oil was a common medical practice in New Testament times. To learn more about this idea, read the following post: RedeemingGod.com/anoint-with-oil-for-healing/

But regardless of whether or not healing occurs, you must not think that the absence of healing means that God is punishing you, has abandoned you, or is just waiting until you have "more faith." Quite to the contrary, when you are sick and injured, God is right there with you, walking through the pain and suffering by your side.

It is so tragic when pastors and preachers tell people who are sick that they were not healed because they didn't have enough faith or that God is punishing them for some sin. Remember that even Paul was not healed by God when he prayed to have the thorn in his flesh removed (2 Cor 12:8).

When you are sick, or when you pray for someone

[1] Oord, *Uncontrolling Love,* 191-216.

else who is sick, feel free to pray for healing. But if the healing does not come, know God is always with you, that He is not punishing you for sin, and that while He wants you to be healed, various unknown circumstances or factors are keeping the healing from occurring. God hates sickness, but a myriad of causes may be stopping God from sending the healing that both He and you want. In such situations, recognize that God is with you, by your side, walking through the pain and suffering, so that your experience can also be used to touch the lives of others who face similar challenges. In this way, while you may not be healed of your disease or sickness, it will be redeemed for God's good purposes.

WHAT ABOUT PRAYING IN TONGUES?

I suppose this is another topic that will require a full book in this Christian Question series. My basic answer, however, goes back to the basic idea I have presented in this book about prayer. When I talk to a friend, I am only going to speak in a way that both of us can understand. If someone is speaking in tongues, then even though God can understand it, the person speaking cannot, let alone anyone else who happens to be listening. So I would say that anyone who desires to speak in tongues should do so only in private settings where they are having a private conversation with God, and even then, it is best to use words that you understand as well.

A longer explanation will have to wait for another book.

WHAT ABOUT PRAYING SCRIPTURE?

I am a big fan of praying with Scripture. This is when you take passages from the Bible and turn them into prayers. I am especially fond of praying the Psalms. Praying the Scriptures in this way allows us to know that we are praying according to the will of God (if we have properly understood the particular text), and also teaches us how biblical authors thought and prayed. You can read something I previously wrote about praying the Psalms here: RedeemingGod.com/praying-the-psalms/

There is a drawback to praying the Scriptures, however. Once again, it all comes back to the idea that prayer is talking to God as you would talk to any other person. If a man wants to speak in romantic ways to his wife, he might be wise to begin by memorizing and reciting some romantic poems to her. But if this is all he ever does, then the romantic poems lose all romance, and they actually will harm the relationship rather than help it.

So also with any other conversation. If you want to talk about sports with a buddy from work, it might be helpful to read a paragraph out of the sports section of the newspaper as a way to get the conversation started, but if all you ever do is read quotes from sports columns, you are not likely to have many meaningful conversations with this other man.

It's the same with praying the Scriptures. Such a practice can be helpful, especially as a way to start a conversation, but if your prayer life consists only (or mostly) of just reading Scriptures to God, your prayer life will never grow or develop, and neither will your relationship with God. Use the Scriptures as prayer training wheels or conversation starters, but don't depend on them to keep the conversation going.

HOW DOES GOD TALK TO US IN PRAYER?

I believe that since prayer is a form of communication with God, this means that God also communicates with us. The problem is that God does not seem to communicate with us the way we communicate with Him. But maybe some of this is because we have not trained ourselves to listen.

So I encourage you to spend more time listening when you pray. You are not listening for an audible voice or anything like that, but for God to impress upon you the things He wants you to do. This might come to you through feelings in your heart, thoughts in your head, or even with something like images, visions, or a still small voice. The difficulty, however, is discerning when such things come from God and when they come from the imaginations of our own heart. Furthermore, this difference is often only realized in hindsight.

Of course, if you want to hear God speak with a little more certainty, the best way is to read Scripture. Since Scripture is God's inspired Word (2 Tim 3:16), this means that Scripture is God breathed, or God spoken, and so God has spoken to you through Scripture, and can even enlighten your mind and encourage your heart through the text of the Bible. While I often find that speaking to God with Scripture is helpful, I find that it is even more helpful to allow God to speak to me through the Scriptures.

But let me issue one warning. Regardless of how you hear the voice of God, never go up to someone else and say, "God told me …" Just don't do it. Make it a rule to live by. If you are right, and God truly did say to you what you want to share, then it will still be true regardless of whether or not you tack on the words, "God told me …"

Furthermore, these three words are little more than spiritual boasting. They are often used by people who want to prove how spiritual they are, or who want to use God's name as a trump card to get people to do what they say. In this latter case, such a use of the words "God told me …" might be taking the Lord's name in vain. If you claim that God is behind something you say, when in fact it is only something that came from your own heart and mind, then you are attaching God's name to something He had nothing to do with in an attempt to give your idea or teachings more credibility.

This is a very dangerous practice to follow. So whether God truly did reveal something to you or not, you don't need to tell people about it.

Ultimately, hearing the voice of God is an important topic, but one which likely cannot be taught. But one thing is certain. If you think you hear God's voice, it will always lead you to act in loving, encouraging, and reconciling ways toward others. It will never be mean or judgmental. If you want to say something mean or judgmental to someone else, don't blame it on God. God's only activity toward humans is to love, heal, and restore, and so when He speaks to us, it will be in ways that encourage us to love, heal, and restore others as well.

Never forget that since God is a God of love, He very often does not tell us what to do, but instead asks us what we want to do. God is not a controlling God. He has given free will to humans, and part of God's journey with humanity is to go with us wherever we go. So the next time you pray, "God, what should I do?" recognize that He might be saying back, "I don't know. What do *you* want to do?" This then creates an opportunity to have a conversation with God about the various available options. Often, God is not as concerned with *what* you do, as much as keeping the lines of communication open with Him *as you do it.*

Here are several blog posts that are related to this topic:

RedeemingGod.com/how-does-god-talk-to-humans/

RedeemingGod.com/how-to-hear-the-voice-of-the-spirit/

RedeemingGod.com/let-me-pray-on-that/

RedeemingGod.com/taking-the-lords-name-in-vain/

DO I NEED TO SAY "AMEN" AT THE END OF MY PRAYERS?

I have a friend who was asked by his pastor to pray over a fellowship meal at church. My friend had not prayed publicly before and was a bit nervous. But he got through the prayer just fine by thanking God for the food and bringing a few requests before Him. Near the end of his prayer, however, he forgot how to "properly conclude" a prayer, and so just said what came natural to him. He said, "Well … goodbye Jesus." Everybody laughed, and he felt a bit ashamed afterwards, but I congratulated him and told him that God probably preferred "Goodbye Jesus" to the traditional ending of "Amen." His concluding words were genuine, and showed that he was talking to God the way he would talk to anyone else. This is exactly what God wants and desires for our prayers.

Many people end their prayers by saying, "Amen." While there is some biblical justification for this practice, the primary reason most follow this practice is because it is tradition. They hear others say "Amen" at the end of their prayers, and so they think that this is how a prayer is supposed to end. Yet I encourage you to stop saying "Amen" at the end of your prayers. I say this for three reasons.

First, it was primarily used in corporate prayer situations, and was primarily spoken by those listening to the prayer, not by those doing the praying. In several of the passages that encourage this practice (cf. Deut 27:15-26; 1 Chr 16:36; Neh 5:13; 8:6), it is not the person praying who says "Amen," but the people listening to the prayer. The practice of saying "Amen" seems to be a practice that was done during corporate prayer rather than private prayer, and was a way for the people to respond to what they were hearing.

But they weren't saying "Amen" just because it was a spiritual thing to say. They had a reason for saying it. This leads to the second reason we can stop saying "Amen" at the end of our prayers. The word "Amen" means "Truly" or "So let it be." When the people in Scripture said "Amen" as part of the corporate prayer, they were simply stating their agreement with what was said. Quite often in prayer meetings, I might find myself nodding my head in agreement or quietly saying the words "Yes" or "Yes, Lord" to what someone else is saying. This is similar to what the people were doing in Scripture when they said "Amen."

Third, saying "Amen" at the "end" of a prayer causes you to think that your prayer is over. I find that when I say "Amen" at the end of a prayer, I subconsciously think that I am done praying. By saying "Amen," I compartmentalize prayer and communication with God into an event that only occurs in specific places at specific times using specific words. But as we have seen in this book, just as an ongoing conversation with a friend or spouse is never over, so also, prayer conversations with God are never over. When you refuse to conclude your prayers with an "Amen," this is a little reminder that your communication with God is ongoing and does not have a beginning or an end.

Nevertheless, despite these three reasons to not say "Amen," there might be one instance where an "Amen" is helpful. This is when you are saying a prayer in front of other people, such as in a church service, a Bible study, or before a meal (but see the question below). In such situations, saying "Amen" is more for them than for God. It helps them know that you are turning from talking to God to talking to them. On the other hand, normal human conversations typically don't provide these sorts of verbal cues to tell others when you are done talking to someone. You just finish your sentence, then turn to the next person you are going to talk to. With a little training, I believe that pastors and Bible study leaders can do the same thing in their prayers. Talk to God with your eyes open, and then simply start talking to the people who are there. I have seen this done in churches and Bible studies from time to time, and I find it quite refreshing. God is treated like another person in the room, and when He is viewed this way, the person teaching the sermon or leading the Bible study then feels the freedom to turn to God again at any time during the service or study to continue the ongoing conversation with Him. In this way, the leader is not only teaching others about Scripture, but is also teaching others about prayer.

Such teaching about prayer through modeling prayer is also something that can be done at home with our children. One great way to do this is during our meals.

DO I NEED TO PRAY OVER MY MEALS?

There are some Scriptures which seem to form the background for the tradition of praying over a meal (Deut 8:10; 1 Tim 4:5; 1 Cor 10:31; Acts 27:35; Matt 14:19-21). But none of these texts specifically command or require that we pray over our meals. God does want us to be mindful of Him when we eat, and to thank Him and give glory to Him for the food He provides to us, but is a perfunctory prayer before we eat really the best way to do this? I am not so sure.

I clearly remember the time when I first began to have second thoughts about the practice of praying over a meal. I was probably about nine or ten and was at a church "Pot-Luck" with my family. My father was one of the pastors and he asked a church elder to say the prayer over the meal. After asking us all to fold our hands, bow our heads, and close our eyes, he said, "God, ... thank you for this food. Amen." Then he raised his head and said, "Let's eat!" I remember being a little startled at such a short prayer. I looked around nervously at the adults and saw some of them glancing at each other with looks that said, "Did that count?" But nobody said anything, and we all started eating. That prayer stuck with me, and it was one of the first times I started questioning why we do what we do in the church, and that there might be a different way to pray than how I had been taught.

Today, my family no longer prays over our meals. I know that this may seem strange to people who grew up with the practice of "Saying Grace" before a meal, but I found that this practice had taught me some bad habits about prayer and I did not want to teach these things to my own children.

Prayers over meals are usually quite formal, repetitive, and perfunctory. Everybody bows their head, folds their hands, closes their eyes, and then one person says some words to God about food and a few other requests, and then closes the prayer with an "Amen" and everybody then promptly forgets about God and moves on with eating the food that is before them. I think it is better to not pray at all over your food than to treat God this way, or to teach others that this is how prayer works.

If you feel that you must pray over your meal, I invite you to keep your head up and your eyes open as you thank God for your food, and then don't say "Amen" at the end of your prayer. Just turn from talking to God to talking to someone else at the table. This helps others see that communication with God is like communication with anyone else.

DO I NEED TO USE WORDS IN MY PRAYERS?

God knows your thoughts, so you do not need to actually verbalize your prayers. You don't need to say them out loud. In fact, you don't really even need to think the words themselves. Many people think that praying is only happening when we say or think words, but since there are numerous forms of communication, I do not believe that words are the only way we can communicate with God.

One form of prayer I have often found to be helpful is what I call picture prayer, or imaging prayer. Though I have used this type of prayer for decades, I recently heard Greg Boyd refer to a similar practice he follows which (if I remember correctly) he referred to as "Imagining Prayer." This form of prayer uses images and pictures in your mind instead of words. When I am praying for a certain situation or person, I find it very helpful to play a little movie in my head or draw a little picture of what I would like to see happen with the situation or person I am praying about. If I had a fight with my wife, rather than ask God for the ability to say I'm sorry, I imagine myself saying "I'm sorry" to my wife, and then hugging and kissing her. When I paint this picture in my head, I am also showing it to God, saying, "This is what I would like to see happen."

I find this approach to prayer to be fun and enjoyable. We all like watching movies, and this form of prayer can be like a movie that you direct in your head. This is especially helpful for people who do not think they are very good "talkers," or who tend to be more creative in their approach to life.

LEARN MORE ABOUT PRAYER

Thank you for reading this book on prayer. If you want to learn more about prayer and how you can grow in your relationship with God by communicating with Him as you would talk to a friend, there are more resources available on my website, RedeemingGod.com

TAKE A COURSE ON PRAYER

If you join my online discipleship group, you can take a course on prayer. The course has seven lessons and is based on the content of this book. There are audio files you can download as well as PDF transcripts, quizzes, and additional recommended resources. Scores of other people have taken this course, which allows you to interact with them in the comment sections of each lesson. I also try to respond to comments in the course lessons, so if you have questions about this book, the comment area might be a good way to connect with me (as well as others who are taking the course).

By taking this course on prayer, the practices and

ideas in this book will be further solidified in your heart and mind, and you will begin to see your relationship with God grow as you learn to speak to Him as you speak to one of your closest friends. Go to RedeemingGod.com/join/ to sign up today. Note that to take this course on prayer, you need to join the Faith, Hope, or Love discipleship levels.

RECEIVE EMAILS ON PRAYER

When you join my online discipleship group, you can also opt in to receive a series of emails on prayer. There are over 20 of these emails, which you will receive weekly. Opt in to receive them by joining any of the four discipleship levels at RedeemingGod.com/join/ (Grace, Faith, Hope, or Love) and then updating your subscription preferences to receive these emails on prayer.

While some of the content of those emails is drawn from this book, there are several emails that contain information not covered by this book or in the course. And as I write more about prayer in the future, I will add it to the content in that email series. So once again, these emails will provide ongoing training, instruction, and encouragement to rethink everything you know about prayer and to put these ideas into practice. Also, if you ever have questions or comments about something you read in these emails, you can simply reply to any of these emails to reach me directly.

ADDITIONAL RESOURCES ON PRAYER

Along with all of the links in the previous chapter, here are some additional online resources which will help you grow in your practice of prayer and your relationship with God.

My Podcast on Jonah 2

I publish a weekly podcast in which we study through books of the Bible. Several episodes of this podcast were devoted to studying the prayer of Jonah in Jonah 2 and his other prayer in Jonah 4. These podcast episodes will be beneficial to you as you consider how (and how not) to pray. Go here to learn more about this podcast and how to subscribe: The One Verse Podcast.

If you want a brief synopsis of what I teach in the podcast, you can read a summary here: The Prayer of Jonah 2.

My Book and Course on the Armor of God

Though it is not yet published, I have written a book on the Armor of God in Ephesians 6:10-20, and will also produce an online course based on this book. As you may know, one major element of the armor of God is the power of prayer (Eph 6:18-20). In fact, prayer is the only "offensive" weapon provided by God for spiritual warfare. The sword of the Spirit is primarily defensive.

If you want to learn more about this book and this course, you can check my booklist or my course list.

These lists will both be updated when the book and course are available. Those who are part of my online discipleship group at RedeemingGod.com/join/ will also be notified when these resources are available.

My Book and Course on *Cruciform Pastoral Leadership*

I have a chapter on prayer in my book, *Cruciform Pastoral Leadership*. As with my other books, I will be producing a course that goes along with this book. The chapter specifically focuses on the role and function of prayer within the life of the church body. It talks about prayer meetings, pastoral prayers, and the prayer life of regular Christians like you and me. There is a bit of overlap between that chapter and this book, but *Cruciform Pastoral Leadership* also contains numerous other suggestions for how pastors and churches can transform their church to better follow Jesus into the world. This book will be part of the "Close Your Church for Good" book series, so while you wait for it to be published you could begin by reading some of the other books that are already available. Start with Volume 1: *The Skeleton Church*.

If you want to learn more about these books and the courses that go with them, you can check my booklist or my course list. All members of my online discipleship group at RedeemingGod.com/join/ can take the course on *The Skeleton Church* for free, and those who join the Faith, Hope, or Love discipleship levels can take all the courses at no additional charge.

ABOUT JEREMY MYERS

Jeremy Myers is an author, blogger, podcaster, and Bible teacher who lives in Oregon with his wife and three daughters. He primarily writes at RedeemingGod.com, where he seeks to help liberate people from the shackles of religion. His site also provides an online discipleship group where thousands of like-minded people discuss life and theology and encourage each other to follow Jesus into the world.

If you appreciated the content of this book, would you consider recommending it to your friends and leaving a review on Amazon? Thanks!

JOIN JEREMY MYERS AND LEARN MORE

Take Bible and theology courses by joining Jeremy at
RedeemingGod.com/join/
Receive updates about free books, discounted books,
and new books by joining Jeremy at
RedeemingGod.com/read-books/

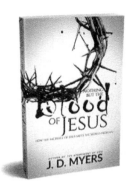

NOTHING BUT THE BLOOD OF JESUS: HOW THE SACRIFICE OF JESUS SAVES THE WORLD FROM SIN

Do you have difficulties reconciling God's behavior in the Old Testament with that of Jesus in the New?

Do you find yourself trying to rationalize God's violent demeanor in the Bible to unbelievers or even to yourself?

Does it seem disconcerting that God tells us not to kill others but He then takes part in some of the bloodiest wars and vindictive genocides in history?

The answer to all such questions is found in Jesus on the cross. By focusing your eyes on Jesus Christ and Him crucified, you come to understand that God was never angry at human sinners, and that no blood sacrifice was ever needed to purchase God's love, forgiveness, grace, and mercy.

In *Nothing but the Blood of Jesus*, J. D. Myers shows how the death of Jesus on the cross reveals the truth about the five concepts of sin, law, sacrifice, scapegoating, and bloodshed. After carefully defining each, this book shows how these definitions provide clarity on numerous biblical texts.

REVIEWS FROM AMAZON

Building on his previous book, 'The Atonement of God', the work of René Girard and a solid grounding in the Scriptures, Jeremy Myers shares fresh and challenging insights with us about sin, law, sacrifice, scapegoating and blood. This book reveals to us how truly precious the blood of Jesus is and the way of escaping the cycle of blame, rivalry, scapegoating, sacrifice and violence that has plagued humanity since the time of Cain and Abel. 'Nothing but the Blood of Jesus' is an important and timely literary contribution to a world desperately in need of the non-violent message of Jesus. –Wesley Rostoll

My heart was so filled with joy while reading this book. Jeremy you've reminded me once more that as you walk with Jesus and spend time in His presence, He talks to you and reveals Himself through the Scriptures. – Amazon Reader

Purchase the eBook for $5.99
Purchase the Paperback for $14.99

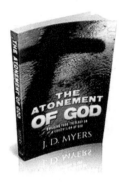

THE ATONEMENT OF GOD: BUILDING YOUR THEOLOGY ON A CRUCIVISION OF GOD

After reading this book, you will never read the Bible the same way again.

By reading this book, you will learn to see God in a whole new light. You will also learn to see yourself in a whole new light, and learn to live life in a whole new way.

The book begins with a short explanation of the various views of the atonement, including an explanation and defense of the "Non-Violent View" of the atonement. This view argues that God did not need or demand the death of Jesus in order to forgive sins. In fact, God has never been angry with us at all, but has always loved and always forgiven.

Following this explanation of the atonement, J. D. Myers takes you on a journey through 10 areas of theology which are radically changed and transformed by the Non-Violent view of the atonement. Read this book, and let your life and theology look more and more like Jesus Christ!

REVIEWS FROM AMAZON

Outstanding book! Thank you for helping me understand "Crucivision" and the "Non-Violent Atonement." Together, they help it all make sense and fit so well into my personal thinking about God. I am encouraged to be truly free to love and forgive, because God has always loved and forgiven without condition, because Christ exemplified this grace on the Cross, and because the Holy Spirit is in the midst of all life, continuing to show the way through people like you. –Samuel R. Mayer

This book gives another view of the doctrines we have been taught all of our lives. And this actually makes more sense than what we have heard. I myself have had some of these thoughts but couldn't quite make the sense of it all by myself. J.D. Myers helped me answer some questions and settle some confusion for my doctrinal views. This is truly a refreshing read. Jesus really is the demonstration of who God is and God is much easier to understand than being so mean and vindictive in the Old Testament. The tension between the wrath of God and His justice and the love of God are eased when reading this understanding of the atonement. Read with an open mind and enjoy! –Clare N. Bez

Purchase the eBook for $4.99

Purchase the Paperback for $11.99

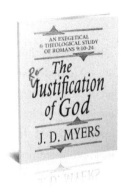

THE RE-JUSTIFICATION OF GOD: A STUDY OF ROMANS 9:10-24

Romans 9 has been a theological battleground for centuries. Scholars from all perspectives have debated whether Paul is teaching corporate or individual election, whether or not God truly hates Esau, and how to understand the hardening of Pharaoh's heart. Both sides have accused the other of misrepresenting God.

In this book, J. D. Myers presents a mediating position. Gleaning from both Calvinistic and Arminian insights into Romans 9, J. D. Myers presents a beautiful portrait of God as described by the pen of the Apostle Paul.

Here is a way to read Romans 9 which allows God to remain sovereign and free, but also allows our theology to avoid the deterministic tendencies which have entrapped certain systems of the past.

Read this book and—maybe for the first time—learn to see God the way Paul saw Him.

REVIEWS FROM AMAZON

Fantastic read! Jeremy Myers has a gift for seeing things from outside of the box and making it easy to understand for the rest of us. The Re -Justification of God provides a fresh and insightful look into Romans 9:10-24 by interpreting it within the context of chapters 9-11 and then fitting it into the framework of Paul's entire epistle as well. Jeremy manages to provide a solid theological exegesis on a widely misunderstood portion of scripture without it sounding to academic. Most importantly, it provides us with a better view and understanding of who God is. If I had a list of ten books that I thought every Christian should read, this one would be on the list. – Wesley Rostoll

I loved this book! It made me cry and fall in love with God all over again. Romans is one of my favorite books, but now my eyes have been opened to what Paul was really saying. I knew in my heart that God was the good guy, but J. D. Myers provided the analysis to prove the text. … I can with great confidence read the difficult chapters of Romans, and my furrowed brow is eased. Thank you, J. D. Myers. I love God, even more and am so grateful that his is so longsuffering in his perfect love! Well done. –Treinhart

Purchase the eBook for $2.99

WHY YOU HAVE NOT COMMITTED THE UNFORGIVABLE SIN: FINDING FORGIVENESS FOR THE WORST OF SINS

Are you afraid that you have committed the unforgivable sin?

In this book, you will learn what this sin is and why you have not committed it. After surveying the various views about blasphemy against the Holy Spirit and examining Matthew 12:31-32, you will learn what the sin is and how it is committed.

As a result of reading this book, you will gain freedom from the fear of committing the worst of all sins, and learn how much God loves you!

REVIEWS FROM AMAZON

This book addressed things I have struggled and felt pandered to for years, and helped to bring wholeness to my heart again. –Natalie Fleming

A great read, on a controversial subject; biblical, historical and contextually treated to give the greatest understanding. May be the best on this subject (and there is very few) ever written. – Tony Vance

You must read this book. Forgiveness is necessary to see your blessings. So if you purchase this book, [you will have] no regrets. –Virtuous Woman

Jeremy Myers covers this most difficult topic thoroughly and with great compassion. –J. Holland

Wonderful explication of the unpardonable sin. God loves you more than you know. May Jesus Christ be with you always. –Robert M Sawin III

Excellent book! Highly recommend for anyone who has anxiety and fear about having committed the unforgivable sin. –William Tom

As someone who is constantly worried that they have disappointed or offended God, this book was, quite literally, a "Godsend." I thought I had committed this sin as I swore against the Holy Spirit in my mind. It only started after reading the verse about it in the Bible. The swear words against Him came into my mind over and over and I couldn't seem to stop no matter how much I prayed. I was convinced I was going to hell and cried constantly. I was extremely worried and depressed. This book has allowed me to breathe again, to have hope again. Thank you, Jeremy. I will read and re-read. I believe this book was definitely God inspired. I only wish I had found it sooner. –Sue

Purchase the eBook for $5.99
Purchase the Paperback for $5.99

SKELETON CHURCH: A BARE-BONES DEFINITION OF CHURCH (PREFACE TO THE CLOSE YOUR CHURCH FOR GOOD BOOK SERIES)

The church has a skeleton which is identical in all types of churches. Unity and peace can develop in Christianity if we recognize this skeleton as the simple, bare-bones definition of church. But when we focus on the outer trappings—the skin, hair, and eye color, the clothes, the muscle tone, and other outward appearances—division and strife form within the church.

Let us return to the skeleton church and grow in unity once again.

REVIEWS FROM AMAZON

I worried about buying another book that aimed at reducing things to a simple minimum, but the associations of the author along with the price gave me reason to hope and means to see. I really liked this book. First, because it wasn't identical to what other simple church people are saying. He adds unique elements that are worth reading. Second, the size is small enough to read, think, and pray about without getting lost. –Abel Barba

In *Skeleton Church*, Jeremy Myers makes us rethink church. For Myers, the church isn't a style of worship, a row of pews, or even a building. Instead, the church is the people of God, which provides the basic skeletal structure of the church. The muscles, parts, and flesh of the church are how we carry Jesus' mission into our own neighborhoods in our own unique ways. This eBook will make you see the church differently. –Travis Mamone

This book gets back to the basics of the New Testament church—who we are as Christians and what our perspective should be in the world we live in today. Jeremy cuts away all the institutional layers of a church and gets to the heart of our purpose as Christians in the world we live in and how to affect the people around us with God heart and view in mind. Not a physical church in mind. It was a great book and I have read it twice now. –Vaughn Bender

The Skeleton Church … Oh. My. Word. Why aren't more people reading this!? It was well-written, explained everything beautifully, and it was one of the best explanations of how God intended for church to be. Not to mention an easy read! The author took it all apart, the church, and showed us how it should be. He made it real. If you are searching to find something or someone to show you what God intended for the church, this is the book you need to read. –Ericka

Purchase the Paperback for $5.99
Purchase the eBook for $2.99

THE DEATH AND RESURRECTION OF THE CHURCH (VOLUME 1 IN THE CLOSE YOUR CHURCH FOR GOOD BOOK SERIES)

In a day when many are looking for ways to revitalize the church, Jeremy Myers argues that the church should die ... so that it can rise again.

This is not only because of the universal principle that death precedes resurrection, but also because the church has adopted certain Satanic values and goals and the only way to break free from our enslavement to these values is to die.

But death will not be the end of the church, just as death was not the end of Jesus. If the church follows Jesus into death, and even to the hellish places on earth, it is only then that the church will rise again to new life and vibrancy in the Kingdom of God.

REVIEWS FROM AMAZON

I have often thought on the church and how its acceptance of corporate methods and assimilation of cultural media mores taints its mission but Jeremy Myers eloquently captures in words the true crux of the matter—

that the church is not a social club for do-gooders but to disseminate the good news to all the nooks and crannies in the world and particularly and primarily those bastions in the reign of evil. That the "gates of Hell" Jesus pronounces indicate that the church is in an offensive, not defensive, posture as gates are defensive structures.

I must confess that in reading I was inclined to be in agreement as many of the same thinkers that Myers riffs upon have influenced me also—Walter Wink, Robert Farrar Capon, Greg Boyd, NT Wright, etc. So as I read, I frequently nodded my head in agreement. –GN Trifanaff

The book is well written, easy to understand, organized and consistent thoughts. It rightfully makes the reader at least think about things as … is "the way we have always done it" necessarily the Biblical or Christ-like way, or is it in fact very sinful?! I would recommend the book for pastors and church officers; those who have the most moving-and-shaking clout to implement changes, or keep things the same. –Joel M. Wilson

Absolutely phenomenal. Unless we let go of everything Adamic in our nature, we cannot embrace anything Christlike. For the church to die, we the individual temples must dig our graves. It is a must read for all who take issues about the body of Christ seriously. –Mordecai Petersburg

Purchase the eBook for $6.99
Purchase the Paperback for $8.99

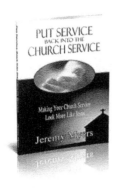

PUT SERVICE BACK INTO THE CHURCH SERVICE (VOLUME 2 IN THE CLOSE YOUR CHURCH FOR GOOD BOOK SERIES)

Churches around the world are trying to revitalize their church services. There is almost nothing they will not try. Some embark on multimillion dollar building campaigns while others sell their buildings to plant home churches. Some hire celebrity pastors to attract crowds of people, while others hire no clergy so that there can be open sharing in the service.

Yet despite everything churches have tried, few focus much time, money, or energy on the one thing that churches are supposed to be doing: loving and serving others like Jesus.

Put Service Back into the Church Service challenges readers to follow a few simple principles and put a few ideas into practice which will help churches of all types and sizes make serving others the primary emphasis of a church service.

Jeremy challenges church addicts, those addicted to an unending parade of church buildings, church services, Bible studies, church programs and more to follow Jesus into our communities, communities filled with lonely, hurting people and BE the church, loving the people in our world with the love of Jesus. Do we need another training program, another seminar, another church building, a remodeled church building, more staff, updated music, or does our world need us, the followers of Jesus, to BE the church in the world? The book is well-written, challenging and a book that really can make a difference not only in our churches, but also and especially in our neighborhoods and communities. –Charles Epworth

I just finished *Put Service Back Into Church Service* by Jeremy Myers, and as with his others books I have read on the church, it was very challenging. For those who love Jesus, but are questioning the function of the traditional brick and mortar church, and their role in it, this is a must read. It may be a bit unsettling to the reader who is still entrenched in traditional "church," but it will make you think, and possibly re-evaluate your role in the church. Get this book, and all others on the church by Jeremy. –Ward Kelly

Purchase the eBook for $5.99
Purchase the Paperback for $5.99

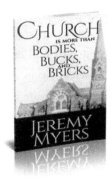

CHURCH IS MORE THAN BODIES, BUCKS, & BRICKS (VOLUME 3 IN THE CLOSE YOUR CHURCH FOR GOOD BOOK SERIES)

Many people define church as a place and time where people gather, a way for ministry money to be given and spent, and a building in which people regularly meet on Sunday mornings.

In this book, author and blogger Jeremy Myers shows that church is more than bodies, bucks, and bricks.

Church is the people of God who follow Jesus into the world, and we can be the church no matter how many people we are with, no matter the size of our church budget, and regardless of whether we have a church building or not.

By abandoning our emphasis on more people, bigger budgets, and newer buildings, we may actually liberate the church to better follow Jesus into the world.

REVIEWS FROM AMAZON

This book does more than just identify issues that have been bothering me about church as we know it, but it goes into history and explains how we got here. In this way it is similar to Viola's *Pagan Christianity*, but I found it a much more enjoyable read. Jeremy goes into more detail on the three issues he covers as well as giving a lot of practical advice on how to remedy these situations. – Portent

This book surprised me. I have never read anything from this author previously. The chapters on the evolution of the tithe were eye openers. This is something that has bothered me for years in the ministry. It may be truth that is too expensive to believe when it comes to feeding the monster. –Karl Ingersoll

Since I returned from Africa 20 years ago I have struggled with going to church back in the States. This book helped me not feel guilty and has helped me process this struggle. It is challenging and overflows with practical suggestions. He loves the church despite its imperfections and suggests ways to break the bondage we find ourselves in. –Truealian

Jeremy Meyers always writes a challenging book ... It seems the American church (as a whole) is very comfortable with the way things are ... The challenge is to get out of the brick and mortar buildings and stagnant programs and minister to the needy in person with funds in hand to meet their needs especially to the widows and orphans as we are directed in the scriptures. –GGTexas

Purchase the eBook for $7.99
Purchase the Paperback for $9.99

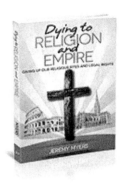

DYING TO RELIGION AND EMPIRE (VOLUME 4 IN THE CLOSE YOUR CHURCH FOR GOOD BOOK SERIES)

Could Christianity exist without religious rites or legal rights? In *Dying to Religion and Empire*, I not only answer this question with an emphatic "Yes!" but argue that if the church is going to thrive in the coming decades, we must give up our religious rites and legal rights.

Regarding religious rites, I call upon the church to abandon the quasi-magical traditions of water baptism and the Lord's Supper and transform or redeem these practices so that they reflect the symbolic meaning and intent which they had in New Testament times.

Furthermore, the church has become far too dependent upon certain legal rights for our continued existence. Ideas such as the right to life, liberty, and the pursuit of happiness are not conducive to living as the people of God who are called to follow Jesus into servanthood and death. Also, reliance upon the freedom of speech, the freedom of assembly, and other such freedoms as established by the Bill of Rights have made the church a servant of the state rather than a servant of God and the gospel. Such freedoms must be forsaken if we are going to live within the rule and reign of God on earth.

This book not only challenges religious and political liberals but conservatives as well. It is a call to leave behind the comfortable religion we know, and follow Jesus into the uncertain and wild ways of radical discipleship. To rise and live in the reality of God's Kingdom, we must first die to religion and empire.

REVIEWS FROM AMAZON

> Jeremy is one of the freshest, freest authors out there—and you need to hear what he has to say. This book is startling and new in thought and conclusion. Are the "sacraments" inviolate? Why? Do you worship at a secular altar? Conservative? Liberal? Be prepared to open your eyes. Mr. Myers will not let you keep sleeping!

> Jeremy Myers is one or the most thought provoking authors that I read, this book has really helped me to look outside the box and start thinking how can I make more sense of my relationship with Christ and how can I show others in a way that impacts them the way that Jesus' disciples impacted their world. Great book, great author. – Brett Hotchkiss

Purchase the eBook for $6.99
Purchase the Paperback for $9.99

CRUCIFORM PASTORAL LEADERSHIP (VOLUME 5 IN THE CLOSE YOUR CHURCH FOR GOOD BOOK SERIES)

This book is forthcoming in early 2017.

The final volume in the *Close Your Church for Good* book series look at issues related to pastoral leadership in the church. It discusses topics such as preaching and pastoral pay from the perspective of the cross.

The best way pastors can lead their church is by following Jesus to the cross!

This book will be published in early 2018.

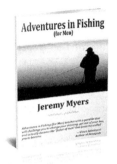

ADVENTURES IN FISHING (FOR MEN)

Adventures in Fishing (for Men) is a satirical look at evangelism and church growth strategies.

Using fictional accounts from his attempts to become a world-famous fisherman, Jeremy Myers shows how many of the evangelism and church growth strategies of today do little to actually reach the world for Jesus Christ.

Adventures in Fishing (for Men) pokes fun at some of the popular evangelistic techniques and strategies endorsed and practiced by many Christians in today's churches. The stories in this book show in humorous detail how little we understand the culture that surrounds us or how to properly reach people with the gospel of Jesus Christ. The story also shows how much time, energy, and money goes into evangelism preparation and training with the end result being that churches rarely accomplish any actual evangelism.

REVIEWS FROM AMAZON

I found *Adventures in Fishing (For Men)* quite funny! Jeremy Myers does a great job shining the light on some of the more common practices in Evangelism today. His allegory gently points to the foolishness that is found within a system that takes the preaching of the gospel and tries to reduce it to a simplified formula. A formula that takes what should be an organic, Spirit led experience and turns it into a gospel that is nutritionally benign.

If you have ever EE'd someone you may find Myers' book offensive, but if you have come to the place where you realize that Evangelism isn't a matter of a script and checklists, then you might benefit from this light-hearted peek at Evangelism today. –Jennifer L. Davis

Adventures in Fishing (for Men) is good book in understanding evangelism to be more than just being a set of methods or to do list to follow. –Ashok Daniel

Purchase the eBook for $0.99

CHRISTMAS REDEMPTION: WHY CHRISTIANS SHOULD CELEBRATE A PAGAN HOLIDAY

Christmas Redemption looks at some of the symbolism and traditions of Christmas, including gifts, the Christmas tree, and even Santa Claus and shows how all of these can be celebrated and enjoyed by Christians as a true and accurate reflection of the gospel.

Though Christmas used to be a pagan holiday, it has been redeemed by Jesus.

If you have been told that Christmas is a pagan holiday and is based on the Roman festival of Saturnalia, or if you have been told that putting up a Christmas tree is idolatrous, or if you have been told that Santa Claus is Satanic and teaches children to be greedy, then you must read this book! In it, you will learn that all of these Christmas traditions have been redeemed by Jesus and are good and healthy ways of celebrating the truth of the gospel and the grace of Jesus Christ.

REVIEWS FROM AMAZON

Too many times we as Christians want to condemn nearly everything around us and in so doing become much like the Pharisees and religious leaders that Jesus encountered. I recommend this book to everyone who has concerns of how and why we celebrate Christmas. I recommend it to those who do not have any qualms in celebrating but may not know the history of Christmas. I recommend this book to everyone, no matter who or where you are, no matter your background or beliefs, no matter whether you are young or old. –David H.

Very informative book dealing with the roots of our modern Christmas traditions. The Biblical teaching on redemption is excellent! Highly recommended. –Tamara

This is a wonderful book full of hope and joy. The book explains where Christmas traditions originated and how they have been changed and been adapted over the years. The hope that the grace that is hidden in the celebrations will turn more hearts to the Lord's call is very evident. Jeremy Myers has given us a lovely gift this Christmas. His insights will lift our hearts and remain with us a long time. –Janet Cardoza

I love how the author uses multiple sources to back up his opinions. He doesn't just use bible verses, he goes back into the history of the topics (pagan rituals, Santa, etc.) as well. Great book! –Jenna G.

Purchase the eBook for $2.99

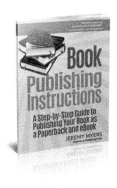

BOOK PUBLISHING INSTRUCTIONS: A STEP-BY-STEP GUIDE TO PUBLISHING YOUR BOOK AS A PAPERBACK AND EBOOK

The dirty little secret of the publishing industry is that authors don't really need publishing companies any longer. If you want to get published, you can!

This book gives you everything you need to take your unfinished manuscript and get it into print and into the hands of readers. It shows you how to format your manuscript for printing as a paperback and preparing the files for digital eReaders like the Kindle, iPad, and Nook.

This book provides tips and suggestions for editing and typesetting your book, inserting interior images, designing a book cover, and even marketing your book so that people will buy it and read it. Detailed descriptions of what to do are accompanied by screenshots for each step. Additional tools, tips, and websites are also provided which will help get your book published.

If you have a book idea, you need to read this book.

REVIEWS FROM AMAZON

I self-published my first book with the "assistance" of a publishing company. In the end I was extremely unhappy for various reasons ... Jeremy Myers' book ... does not try to impress with all kinds of "learned quotations" but gets right to the thrust of things, plain and simple. For me this book will be a constant companion as I work on a considerable list of books on Christian doctrines. Whether you are a new aspiring author or one with a book or so behind you, save yourself much effort and frustration by investing in this book.
–Gerrie Malan

This book was incredibly helpful. I am in the process of writing my first book and the info in here has really helped me go into this process with a plan. I now realize how incredibly naive I was about what goes into publishing a book, yet instead of feeling overwhelmed, I now feel prepared for the task. Jeremy has laid out the steps to every aspect of publishing step by step as though they were recipes in a cook book. From writing with Styles and using the Style guide to incorporating images and page layouts, it is all there and will end up saving you hours of time in the editing phase. –W. Rostoll

Purchase the eBook for $9.99
Purchase the Paperback for $14.99

THE LIE – A SHORT STORY

When one billion people disappear from earth, what explanation does the president provide? Is he telling the truth, or exposing an age-old lie?

This fictional short story contains his televised speech.

Have you ever wondered what the antichrist will say when a billion people disappear from planet earth at the rapture? Here is a fictional account of what he might say.

Purchase the eBook for $0.99

JOIN JEREMY MYERS AND LEARN MORE

Take Bible and theology courses by joining Jeremy at
RedeemingGod.com/join/

Receive updates about free books, discounted books, and new books by joining Jeremy at
RedeemingGod.com/read-books/

Made in the USA
Las Vegas, NV
17 January 2022

41651544R00098